PLANES & PILOTS

# Mikoyan-Gurevitch
# MIG
## 15 & 17
### FAGOT, MIDGET & FRESCO

GÉRARD PALOQUE
*Translated from the French by Alan McKay*

*Histoire & Collections*

# The MiG-15 ('Fagot')

Like all the main western countries, the USSR had started to work on various projects for jet-powered aircraft even before the Second World War was over. It was in response to an official request for a jet-powered plane made as early as February 1945 that the MiG OKB (*Opytnoye Konstuktorskoye Buro* – the design office) responded with the I-300 (or *Izdeliye* – model – F) prototype, of which the first of three examples flew on 28 April 1946. Powered by two RD-20 jet engines (BMW 003 copies) installed under the fuselage, the machine – called the MiG-9 ('Fargo' in the NATO nomenclature [1]) when it made its first public appearance during the official fly past over the Red Square in Moscow the following November – entered service with the V-VS (*Voenno-Vozduchnye Sily*, the Soviet Air Force) in 1947 and in the end more than 700 examples were built.

Like its contemporaries the Sukhoi Su-9 which looked very much like the Messerschmitt Me 262, and the Yak-15 and Yak-17 ('Feather'), the MiG-9 used not very powerful jet engines developed directly in the USSR and copied especially from the German Jumo 004 and BMW 003 engines of which a large stock had been captured after the war, together with some of the engineers that had built them...

As this mediocre engine performance had to be dealt with, it was decided that the Vladimir Yakovlevitch Klimov design bureau located in the Leningrad (now St Petersburg) suburbs, would be given the task of making copies of the most modern jet engine of the period, the Rolls Royce Nene [2]. This task was made all the easier when the British labour Government officially provided the Russians with thirty Nene Is (rated at 4 906 lb st./2 230 kgp) and Nene IIs (rated at 4 884 lb st/2 270 kgp), and thirty Derwent 5s (rated at 3 498 lb st/1 590 kgp), along with all the plans and information they needed for building them under licence. These engines were immediately built by the Soviets under the designations RD-45 [3], RD-45F and RD-500.

A MiG-9FR, the last variant of the first production series jet fighter built by the MiG OKB.

---

1. Under the NATO coding system set up just after the Second World War by the ASCC (Air Standardisation Coordinating Committee), Soviet machines were given an English code-name whose initial letter indicated what they were: F for fighters (Fagot, Fishbed, etc.), M for trainers (Midget, Mongol, etc.), H for helicopters (Hind, Hip, Hoplite, etc.), and so on.
2. The centrifugal flow Nene was less effective than the German axial flow jets but was more reliable because it was built using more solid materials, and especially it was easier to build.

## Project Development

During an official conference in March 1946 assembling all the main fighter aircraft builders, before the MiG-9s and the Yak-17s and even the new jet engines were built, Stalin asked the Yakovlev, MiG and Lavotchkin design teams to design a daytime fighter capable of using summarily prepared airstrips and able to intercept enemy bombers flying at high altitudes (36000 ft). For this, the plane had to be able to climb very fast, to fly at Mach 0.9 and remain in the air for at least an hour. The future fighter also had to be able to carry out ground attacks as well as its main task.

The swept wing layout was considered to be more or less unavoidable, especially if the research carried out by the TsAGI (*Tsentral'nyy Aerodiamicheshki i Gidrodinamischeskiy Institut* – the central aerohydrodynamics institute) was to be put into practice; they had been studying swept wing concepts since 1935, and particularly those developed by captured German engineers.

In response to this official request, Lavotchkin put forward his La-168, a variant of his La-160 with sweptback wings which ended up as the La-15 ('Fantail'), of which only a few were built, and Yakovlev the Yak-30, derived from the Yak-25; both machines were powered by the Rolls Royce Derwent copy, the RD-500, which the aircraft builders had chosen because it was lighter (1 243 lb/565 kg) and much more suitable for their lightweight fighters.

As for the MiG OKB, it decided to choose the RD-45, somewhat heavier (1 584 lb/720 kg) than its counterparts but also more powerful, at the same time designing a totally new aircraft. The project was headed by the engineers A.G. Brunov and A.A. Andreyev, aided by a team from the TsAGI, who at first envisaged using various wing types (swept back, swept forward or straight) all of which were tested in the TsAGI wind tunnel.

In March 1947, the sweptback wing fitted with fences to channel the air flow appeared to be the best compromise, the ideal angle of the wings being fixed at 35% to 25% of the cord, with a 2° negative dihedral at the wing roots.

Officialised in February 1947 as the "Plane S" (S for Strelovidnost – arrow) from MiG, designed by the NII (Nauchno-Issledovatel'skii Institut – research institute) I-310, it won the final official competition and an order was placed for several prototypes.

## From prototype to production series

The MiG OKB at first built two prototypes of its future fighter, S-01 and S-02. The first was fitted with an original Nene engine and flew for the first time on 30 December 1947 with Viktor Yuganov at the controls. The trials were quickly broken off because the engine lost power. To remedy this, it was decided to shorten the rear of the fuselage and the tip of the exhaust pipe slightly, modifications which themselves led to other modifications: increased sweep to 40° for the horizontal tail surfaces, redesigned flaps and ailerons; and enlarged tail fin surface.

The S-02 was powered by the more powerful Nene II (4 994 lb/2 270 kg) and made its maiden flight six months later on 27 May 1948 flown by Colonel Grigory Sedov. Shortly earlier, MiG had brought out a third prototype, the S-03, which took into account all the modifications made to the other two during the trials. The overall structure of the plane was reinforced and the outer skin, made of a different alloy, was thicker whilst the ailerons were enlarged by increasing the surface of the flaps. Airbrakes operated by hydraulic jacks were added to the rear of the fuselage, the area of the ailerons were increased to make them more effective; the size of the flaps was reduced (but with a bigger cord), and the horizontal tail surfaces were moved backwards 6 inches (150 mm) compared with the original ones which meant that the tail fin had to be revised.

Moreover there were strong points under the wings, to take drop tanks for 109 gallons (496 l) of extra fuel or various offensive loads and new equipment was fitted in particular ASP-1N sights and an S-13 camera gun.

Having flown the first time on 17 June 1948, the S-03 reached Mach 0.93 during its test flights, with its defects being eliminated one by one. However, as the first flights had shown the plane tended to go into a spin during tight bends it was decided to limit its speeds to Mach 0.92, with the airbrakes coming out automatically as soon as it reached Mach 0.91. As the MiG prototypes turned out to be far better than their rivals, it was decided during a meeting of the ministers in August 1948 to start series production of the I-310, officially named the MiG-15 with the Commander-in-Chief accepting the new model on 23 December 1948.

---
3. Because it was produced at the N°45 factory ('Zavod' in Russian) in Moscow.

Above:
One of the features of the MiG-15 (then the MiG-17) was its armament installed on a tray which could be easily removed from the fuselage, fastened by four cables.

### MiG-15 (MiG-15Bis) SPECIFICATIONS

**Type**
Single-seat turbo-jet-powered interceptor
**Powerplant**
One centrifugal Klimov RD-45F turbojet rated at 4 994 lb st (2 270 kgp) dry [MiG-15bis: one VK-1 rated at 5 940 lb st (2 700 kgp)]
**Dimensions**
Wingspan: 33 ft (10.08 m)
Overall length: 33 ft 1 ½ in (10.10 m)
Height: 12 ft 1 ½ in (3.70 m)
Wing surface: 221.717 ft² (20.60 m²)
Weight (empty): 7 157 lb (3 253 kg) [8 096 lb (3 680 kg)]
Max. take off weight: 11 891 lb (5 405 kg) [12 172 lb (5 533 kg)]
**Performances**
Max. Speed: 644 mph (1 031 kph) at 16 400 ft (5 000 m); 656 mph (1 050 kph) at sea level. [671 mph (1 075 kph)]
Rate of climb: 16 400 ft (5 000 m) in 2 ½ minutes [1.95 minutes]; 26 240 ft (8 000 m) in 5 minutes; 32 800 ft (10 000 m) in 7.1 minutes [4.9 minutes]
Operational ceiling: 50 840 ft (15 500 m)
Range: 734 miles (1 175 km) or 1 031 miles (1 650 km) with drop tanks. [1 015 miles (1 625 km)]
Take-off run: 2 066 ft (630 m) [1 558 ft (475 m)]
Landing run: 2 361 ft (720 m) [2 197 ft (670 m)]
**Armament**
One 37 mm 40-round N-37D canon and two 23-mm 80-round NR-23 cannon.

## In the units

Produced first at the GAZ (*Gosudarstvenny Aviatsionyy Zavod* – state aviation factory) N°1, deliveries of the MiG-15 – known at first by the name of SV (for arrow/air force) – to the operational units of the PVO (*Protivo-Vozdushnaya Oborona*, anti-aircraft defence force) started from October 1948 onwards.

Compared with the prototypes, the production series machines were slightly different: RD-45F engine (in fact a Nene II built under licence), reinforced structure with internal modifications, NR-23 instead of NS-23 cannon, new shock absorber for the nose wheel undercarriage leg and ASP-3N sights in place of the ASP-1 ones.

Besides that, improvements were constantly made to the plane throughout its production: increased airbrake surface area, reinforced pilot protection, faired drop tanks compatible with the high speeds reached by the fighter, and a landing light fitted into the front air intake splitter. The following year, on 20 May 1949, the USSR's Council of Ministers decided to increase fighter production on larger scale, so much so that it was decided to stop making out-of-date models (La-15, Li-2, Yak-17 and 23) and use their factories solely for MiG-15 production now considered a priority.

## In service

Called 'Falcon' initially by NATO then shortly afterwards 'Fagot', the MiG-15 made its first official appearance during the 1 May 1949 flypast when a group of 45 fighters flew over the Red Square. Deliveries to operational Soviet units started during the following winter and the MiG-15 was quickly sent to Korea to take part in the conflict which broke out between the north and the south of the country on 25 June 1950.

## Technical aspects of the MiG-15

The new fighter was characterised by the care taken in ensuring the pilot was comfortable, with pressurised cockpit and air conditioning, ejector seat and tear drop canopy. With good performances due to its optimal wing loading, it had an excellent weight to power ratio; its armament maintenance was simple and servicing the reliable RD-45 engine was made all the easier by the fact that the rear part of the

Below:
On 21 September 1953, Lieutenant Kum-Sok No, of the North Korean Air Force defected with his MiG-15 and landed at Kimpo AB. The fighter was thoroughly evaluated, especially by the famous Chuck Yeager. (USAF)

Above: a tract promising a reward to any pilot delivering a MiG to the Allies. (USAF)

Rare colour photo of No Kum-Sok's MiG-15, just a few moments after landing at Kimpo, alongside a Sabre of the 4th Fighter Wing. (USAF)

A frequent shot taken during the Korean War: the last moments of a Fagot, taken by an American Sabre's camera gun. (USAF)

fuselage could be completely removed by simply undoing four bolts located near frame N°13.

The plane's silhouette was greatly inspired by wartime research carried out by the Germans and closely resembled that of the Focke-Wulf Ta 183 with its T-shaped tail, comprising a swept back fin and especially its swept back horizontal tail surfaces located mid-way up the fin with a 40° sweep. The swept back wings (35°) with a very slight negative dihedral (2°) had two fences on each wing designed to regulate the flow of air on the surfaces to give the controls all possible effect. The tricycle undercarriage comprised a nose wheel which retracted into a well fitted in the partition splitting the air intake, and the main undercarriage consisting of a single wheel retracted flat into the wing. All the fuel was carried in the fuselage in nonrigid but protected tanks.

The RD-45 centrifugal turbojet rated at 5005 lb s.t. (20275 kgp) was fed by an air intake in the front of the fuselage split in two by a partition housing the nosewheel well.

The armament envisaged initially was replaced in the end by a novel system comprising a 'tray' containing weapons, magazines and shell link extractor, which could be lowered for maintenance using a winch linked to four cables by means of pulleys. The MiG-15's armament comprised an N-37D 37-mm 40-round canon housed on the right hand side and two 80-round 23-mm NR-23s situated on the left, all these weapons firing on the same horizontal plane.

## The MiG-15UTI two-seater

The need for a two-seater version of the MiG-15 to familiarise pilots who up until then had only flown piston-engined planes appeared as soon as the plane went through its first trials in 1947, particularly as the plane's handling turned out to be particularly demanding for novice pilots. The construction project however was only launched on 13 April 1949 by official decree. At the time, studies carried out by the MiG OKB concerning this UTI (*Uchebno Trenirovich Istrebitel* – formation and training fighter) were so complete that production was able to start quickly.

Apart from the front part of the fuselage which had to be modified to carry the second pilot, which meant reducing the amount of fuel carried in this section of the plane, the two-seater was similar to the standard MiG-15. In order to speed up transition, the two cockpits were identical (instrument panels, ejector seats – the rear one ejecting first) and the windshield had been heightened. The movable parts of the canopy opened differently, the front one swinging over to the right and the rear one sliding backwards as on the single-seater. The second seat reduced the amount of fuel carried, but the plane could still carry extra fuel in the underwing drop tanks.

To save space, the armament had been simplified. The first series were indeed armed with a 12.7-mm 150-round UBK-E machine gun and an 80-round NR-23 canon only on the left. This second weapon was quickly suppressed (after N° 10444) and sometimes replaced by an instrument landing system.

The MiG-15UTI ('Midget' for NATO) prototype took to the air for the first time on 23 May 1949 and after its trials, series production was launched in the following September. The two-seater was built in only one factory, devoted entirely to producing the more than 6500 examples built, a small number of which was built abroad and the type continued to serve well after the single-seater had been withdrawn, right up until the end of the 20th century. For instance, from 1952 onwards, each Soviet fighter regiment had at least four MiG-15UTIs used mainly for training the pilots of other MiG fighters, mainly the MiG-17 of which no two-seat version was ever produced in the USSR. Apart from this vital task, the 'Midget' was also used for weather reconnaissance and several types of training: blind flying, night or bad weather, or even bombing since it still had the underwing pylons carrying two FAB-50 or -100 bombs.

## The MiG-15bis

As Klimov, the engine builder, had designed a better version of his centrifugal turbojet, the VK-1 (for Vladimir Klimov), rated at 5 940 lb st (2 700 kgp), it was decided to fit it inside the MiG-15 airframe whose original dimensions meant it didn't have to be modified. However, the increase in power and therefore in the plane's performances, meant the wings had to be reinforced and the airbrakes (whose surface area was increased from 0.5 to 0.8 m²) and the tail redesigned.

The fuel capacity was also increased (from 275 gallons/1 250 l to 310 gallons/1 410 l) and the ailerons were equipped with a BU-1 servo motor, a first for an aircraft designed by MiG. The windshield was armoured and some of the machines were equipped with an OSP-48 instrument landing system making night time flying possible. As for the wing tanks, they were replaced by faired models containing 88 gallons (400 l) which could be mounted on either side which was not the case with the earlier pairs. Even though the MiG-15bis came off the production lines with the same armament as the MiG-15, this was improved during the production run. Whilst the N-37 37-mm canon was retained on the right hand side, two N-23 23-mm cannon replaced the N-23s installed up until then. These weapons had an improved feed system, a greater rate of fire (400 rounds per minute) and their shells had a greater muzzle velocity.

The wings had four hard points on which a whole range of weapons (for example, two 55-gallon (250 l) tanks and two 110 lb (50 kg) or 220 lb (100 kg) bombs) could be attached. In fact the MiG-15 – whatever version – was not really suited to ground attack missions, first of all because its offensive load was rather limited, but above all because the plane was not equipped with a suitable set of sights: it let off a salvo of shells just before launching its unguided rockets.

The MiG-15bis ('Fagot B' – the standard MiG-15 became the 'Fagot A' retroactively) entered service in the V-VS at the end of 1950 and was in turn quickly deployed in Korea where its powerful armament and its good handling came as a nasty surprise for the United Nations forces and it turned out to be far superior to all the Allied fighters of the time, and especially the USAF's F-80s and F-84s, and the US Navy's F9F Panthers and F2H Banshees, particularly where acceleration, turning circle and offensive load were concerned.

The Allies had to wait for the arrival of the F-86E, an improved version of the famous Sabre [4] for the MiG to have a worthy adversary. Although designed for different tasks – the MiG-15 for intercepting bomber boxes and therefore equipped with powerful slow rate of fire cannon, and the F-86 Sabre, a pure fighter equipped with only small calibre (12.7 mm) machine guns but firing faster – the two planes were very similar and it was the skill of the pilots that made all the difference. Although the USAF pilots scored a high number of kills in Korea it was mainly because they were faced most of the time with less skilled adversaries, the North-Korean or Chinese pilots replacing their Soviet colleagues during the conflict not being up to their American opponents who were far better trained.

The MiG-15bis only remained in service with the Soviet Air Force until the very beginning of the 1950s when they were replaced in front line service by more effective fighters, like the MiG-17 to begin with. Although the two-seat version had a much longer career especially abroad, the 'Fagot' was still in service, in small numbers in several Middle Eastern countries, like Egypt and Syria in 1967, even though at the time they were kept for ground attack missions and most of them were destroyed on the ground anyway by the Israeli Air Force in the first hours of the Six-Day War.

# Versions and variants

Although the MiG-15 and then the MiG-15bis were constantly improved all throughout their production, with feedback from the users themselves being taken into account, they did give rise to several specialised variants which were produced in limited quantities, or even prototypes for which there was no production series. Among the mains ones were:

— MiG-15Sbis (factory designation: SD-UPB): long-range escort fighter for the Il-28 and Tu-14 bombers, able to carry an extra 132 gallon (600 l) drop tank under each (specially reinforced) wing, giving a range of 1 562 miles (2 500 km) at 39 360 ft (12 000 m), with increased oxygen supply for the pilot. At least fifty or so of this variant were produced at the beginning of 1951.

---

4. For a while when the MiG-15 appeared over Korea, there were rumours that it was nothing but a copy of the Sabre whose plans had been stolen by Communist spies. Obviously the truth was totally different: the similarity between the two planes was due to the fact that they both originated from the same wartime research carried out by the Germans, particularly on the Ta 183.

Below:
MiG-15UTI of the HavLv 31 of the Suomen Ilmavoimat – the Finnish Air Force.

Above:
Czech Air Force Aero CS-102 (MiG-15UTI) in flight.

— MiG-15Rbis (SR or SR-1): photo reconnaissance version with one of the N-23 cannon replaced by an AFA/BA camera and an improved cockpit air conditioning and insulation system.

— MiG-15Pbis (SP-1): all-weather fighter with a longer fuselage, a radome situated on the upper air intake lip, a modified nose wheel, and armament reduced to a single canon on the right hand side. This model, of which two prototypes and five demonstration examples were produced, was tried out in December 1949 but turned out to be disappointing, in particular regarding the 'Toriy' (Thorium) radar; in the end it was never series produced for lack of official certification.

— MiG-15Pbis (SP-5): prototype fitted with an 'Izumrud' (emerald) RP-1 radar with an antenna fitted in a radome situated over the air intake. Armament reduced to two NR-23 cannon with 120 rounds (right hand gun) and 90 rounds (left hand gun). Despite satisfactory trials, this version was not series produced either, this radar type being installed on the MiG-17 all-weather fighter version.

Finally among the aircraft that were specially modified as flying test beds, it's worth mentioning the MiG-15SU armed with two pivoting 23-mm cannon located under the fuselage; the MiG-15bis ISh ground attack version with under wing pylons for carrying faired loads; and the 'Fagots' equipped with a boom for in-flight refuelling, or equipped with a system (nicknamed 'Burlaki' in memory of the boatmen from the Tsarist period) enabling them to be towed in flight with engines shut down behind a Tu-4 (the copy of the American B-29).

## Licence built production

Although the USSR was, not surprisingly, the main builder of the 'Fagot' (more than 13 000 examples, among which 1 350 MiG15s, 8200 MiG-15bis and 3 400 MiG-15UTIs) the fighter was also built in large numbers under licence by several countries which in turn sold them abroad.

In Czechoslovakia the national aircraft manufacturer, Avia, produced the MiG-15 under the designation **S-102** (821 or 853 examples according to the sources) from 1953 to 1955 in its Vodochody factory. The first example took off for the first time on 13 April 1953 and was followed by the CS-102 (MiG-15UTI, 620 ex.) and by the **S-103** (MiG-15bis, 620 ex.). These machines were fitted with a locally made jet engine designed by Motorlet. Since the Czech engineering industry had acquired a long-standing reputation for excellence, the 'Fagots' and 'Midgets' made in this country were thought to be the best ones ever to come off the production lines. These machines were used by a lot of 'friendly' countries, including the USSR itself then later, second hand, by various African, Middle Eastern and Asian countries.

It was in fact Poland, at WSK's Mielec factory, that built the MiG-15 first under licence, from 1952 onwards, the first machines being initially assembled on the spot from parts supplied by Russia; the Mielec factory's job was to build the different versions of the MiG-15 under licence, the engines being made at the WSK Rzezow factory and called Lis-1 (RD-45F) and Lis-2 (VK-1). The first version, the **Lim-1** (for *Licencyjny mysliwie* – licence built fighter) was the equivalent of the MiG-15 and was built from 1952 to 1957 (227 ex.).

It was followed by the **Lim-2** (MiG-15bis), built from 1954 to 1956 (about 500 ex.). Based on these the following models were subsequently produced: the Lim1.5, a standard MiG-15, transformed into a 'bis'; the **Lim-2R**, a reconnaissance version carrying an AFA-21 camera in a fairing under the fuselage; and the **SBLim-1** and **SBLim-2**: Lim-1s and -2s hastily converted into two seaters at the end of the fifties and which only retained a single MR-23 canon. Although a big user of the MiG-15/15bis, China never produced the single seat version under licence (although it was known locally as the Shenyang **J-2** – the Shenyang factory built with Russian help only being used to repair damaged planes). On the other hand it did produce a large number of two-seaters under the designations **JJ-2** and **FT-2** for export.

Below:
An Aero S-103, the licence-built version of the MiG-15bis produced in Czechoslovakia. (DR)

# The MiG-17 ('FRESCO')

As early as 1949, it was decided to have part of the team that had designed the MiG-15 start designing its immediate successor, designated I-330 (or *Izdeliye SI* – 'improved sweep'). In March of the same year, the MiG OKB was given permission to build an airframe, the SI-1, to be used in static trials, and two others for active trials, the SI-2 and SI-3, the two machines being also designated unofficially the "MiG-15bis-45", the 45 referring to the increased sweep given to the wings.

The SI-1 flew for the first time on 23 January 1950 and reached Mach 1.03 (1 114 kph) in level flight on the following 1 February before it was lost in an accident which cost the pilot his life on 20 March. Two pre-production series machines, SI-01 and SI-02, were therefore built and SI-03 never flew. SI-02 was the first to be tested in 1951, the year in which the plane was finally given its official designation, MiG-17.

Compared with the MiG-15bis from which it derived (identical cockpit layout, undercarriage, armament and avionics), the new MiG-17 could be recognised by its modified wings (with a double sweep back – 49° on the first half of the wing and 45° on the second, with a greater surface area but reduced wingspan – and a 3° negative dihedral), and its enlarged flaps, airbrakes and tail unit. The amount of fuel carried was identical and the rear part of the fuselage had been lengthened by 36 in (90 cm), with armament and wing pylons unchanged.

As stipulated in a Council of Ministers decision taken in August 1951, series production of the new machine was to start officially on 1 September, i.e. even before the tests had been completed, since the five factories whose job was to build it had previously produced the MiG-15. The first production series machines came off the production line at the beginning of 1952 and were delivered to a fighter regiment based in Crimea given the task of carrying out the operational trials. Once it was known to the West, the type was given the code name 'Fresco' by NATO (then 'Fresco A', as and when new variants were put into service).

## First version, first modifications

As had happened with the MiG-15, the MiG-17 never stopped being improved all throughout its production. The first production series examples were fitted with a VK-1A engine with the same thrust (5 940 lb st/2 700 kgp) which was more reliable and had a longer life span; the wingspan was increased and two ventral fins added, the only things enabling one

The SI-1, the first prototype of the I-330, the future MiG-17.

to distinguish a MiG-15 from a MiG-17 whose silhouettes were otherwise very similar. A new more effective ejector seat was also installed and the landing light was moved to the left-hand wing air intake. The canopy no longer had any supports, a periscope was added to improve rearwards vision and faired 88 gallon (400 l) drop tanks could be carried underwing. As it became rapidly apparent that the air brakes were not effective enough, they were modified several times until they reached their final trapezoidal shape, their surface area being increased to 0.88 m². The first production series MiG-17s were able to reach Mach 1.14 and deliveries to the V-VS started in October 1952.

In all, about 8 000 examples of this version were made, not counting those made under licence abroad, especially in Poland or in China.

# The MiG-17F (SF) 'Fresco C'

This version featured a VK-1F engine rated at 7 436 lb st (3 380 kgp) with afterburner and an exhaust pipe fitted with six nozzle slats; it started its trials at the end of September 1951. Apart from the new powerplant, its rear fuselage had been shortened, its airbrakes had been enlarged again (0.97 m² surface area), and its rudder cord was more marked.

Since series production had started at the end of 1952, deliveries of the MiG-17F started in February 1953 and the older models of the fighter then in service in front line VVS units were replaced. Its performances were better than those of the first version since the MiG-17F could fly at Mach 0.99 at 11000m. Its armament consisted one 40-round N-37D and two 80-round N-23 cannon, and two bombs (110, 220 or 550 lb/50, 100 or 250 kg) could be slung under the wings, as well as two 88 gall. (400 l) drop tanks (occasionally 132 gall./600 l).

Although the MiG-17 entered service while the Korean War was still being fought, it did not take part in it, perhaps because Stalin himself vetoed it. Like its predecessor, it was also built in China and Poland, certain examples intended for export being modified in the sixties so they could fire the R-3S air to air missile (AA-2-2 – 'Advanced Atoll').

# The MiG-17P (SP-7) 'Fresco B'

Two variants of the MiG-17 were originally intended: a standard daytime fighter and an all-weather night fighter. Indeed a prototype designated SP-2 was fitted with a 'Korshun' (kite) radar which was in fact a development of the 'Toriy' used earlier on the MiG-15bis. Apart from the addition of a radome in the upper part of the air intake lip, the armament on this machine was modified by removing the on-board 37-mm canon.

As had been the case several months earlier, the pilot operating the radar alone was thought to be too complicated and the SP-2 did not go into production. The trials however were continued this time with an RP-1 'Izumrud' radar ('Scan ODD' in the NATO nomenclature) installed in five trial machines in 1952. The two antennae were installed in the same way as on the 'Fagot': the search antenna in a flat, oblong fairing on a level in the extended lip over the intake, and the pursuit antenna in the intake dividing wall. The instruments were also changed, with a screen added to the instrument panel, whilst the 37-mm canon was replaced by a third 23-mm NR-23, each of these weapons having 100 rounds. As the trials of these machines turned out to be conclusive, series production of this version called the MiG-17P (P for *Perekhvahtchik* – interceptor and 'Fresco B' for NATO) was given the go-ahead during the summer of 1953, with the aircraft, the first single-seaters to be equipped with radar to see service in the USSR, being delivered mainly to units of the PVO and the Navy.

# The MiG-17PF (SP-7/7F) 'Fresco D'

This version, whose prototype flew for the first time in August 1952, was in fact a MiG-17P powered by a VK-1F fitted with afterburners; it had undergone several modifications such as the addition of a 'Sirena 2' radar alert detector (installed on a Soviet aircraft for the first time) and an NI-50B ground positioning system; the airbrakes were those of the MiG-17F with a bigger surface area (0.88 m²).

Produced in series in 1953, the MiG-17PF underwent some improvements during its career and the last examples that came off the production lines (Izdeliye SP-7F) the following year were equipped for instance with a better Izumrud 2 RP-5 radar, recognisable by its radome positioned on the bigger intake dividing wall. In the middle of the fifties, a small number of MiG-17PFs were equipped with the Gorizont-1 ground station guidance system and for this were renamed MiG-17PFG (for *Gorizont*).

About a thousand MiG-17PFs were delivered to the PVO, those still in service in 1956 being transformed into MiG-17PFUs.

## The MiG-17PFU (SP-15) 'Fresco E'

At the end of 1956 when the MiG-19 went into service, a batch of MiG-17PFs was specially modified (radar and firing system) so they could carry the K-5 (RS-2/AA-1 'Alkali') air to air missile. For this two missile APU-4 launchers were installed under each wing on the leading edge, inboard of the drop tank pylon; all the on-board cannon were removed.

The MiG-17PFU (U standing for *Usovershenstvovanny* – improved) was the first fighter to be armed with missiles but only a limited number were built, used only by the PVO from the middle of 1955 onwards. At the end of their career, at the end of the fifties, the surviving Fresco Es were used to train MiG-19 and 21 pilots.

## Test beds

As with the MiG-15, the main versions of MiG-17 were constantly being updated while it was being produced. As well as modifications made to the production series machines, a large number of Frescoes were used for all sorts of trials, some of which ended up being production series and others not.

For instance, the front part of a MiG-17, the 'Izdeliye SN', was substantially modified to house three pivoting N-23 cannon, and the air intakes moved to the sides. Another plane, the 'Izdeliye SM-1' (or I-340), was equipped with two jet engines placed side by side in the rear of the fuselage which had had to be widened. This prototype, which flew in the spring of 1952, performed better than a standard 'Fresco' since it was able to go through the sound barrier in level flight, but no production series was ever made because the engines were unreliable.

Various armament tests (installing rocket launchers in the nose, carrying the 'Kennel' KS-1/AS-1 antishipping missile or installing double cannon for the on-board armament) or equipment tests (radar or in-flight refuelling probes) were also carried out at the beginning of the fifties, whilst at the end of their operational career, a large number of MiG-17s were used as drones or flying targets under the designations MiG-17M or MM.

Below:
This Syrian MiG-17F landed in open country during the Six-Day War and was captured by the Israelis.

## Built under licence

At the beginning of the fifties, China received a certain number of MiG-17s which it renamed **J-4** and **F-4** when the machines were sold on for export. In 1955, it obtained the design plans for the MiG-17F off Russia as well as two examples to be used as models for series production together with the parts for a further 15 machines and the elements to make ten others. The first MiG-17F made in China in the Shenyang factory under the designation **J-5** (**F-5** for export) took to the air on 19 July 1956. Licen-

Below:
Lim-5 from the 39. PLM of the Polish Air Force. This is the MiG-17 version built under licence in Poland by WSK-PZL.

The sole 'Izdeliye SN' equipped with swinging cannons in a deeply modified front fuselage.

sed production of the MiG17PF turned out to be more complicated since although the plans were obtained in 1961, the first production series machine, called **J-5A** (F-5A for export) only flew in 1964, when the type was already out of date. However, more than 750 J-5s and J-5As were built up to 1969, when the production lines were shut down. Although the USSR had not considered it necessary to produce a two-seat version of the Fresco, China produced it under the designation **JJ-5** (FT-5). It was in fact a mix of several models with the MiG-15UTI's internal layout, the MiG-17's engine without afterburner, the MiG-17F's airbrakes, and an upper lip on the air intake similar to that of the MiG-17PF even though it didn't house any radar. Armed only with one 23-mm canon, the first two-seater produced by the Chengdu factory (more than 1 000 ex.) flew in 1968 and was very

## MiG-17F SPECIFICATIONS

**Powerplant**
1 Klimov VK-1F turbojet rated at 7 480 lb st (3 400 kg) thrust with after burning.
**Dimensions**
Length: 36 ft 4 in (11.09 m)
Height: 12 ft 6 in (3.80 m)
Wingspan: 31 ft 6 in (9.63 m)
Wing surface: 243.24 ft² (22.60 m²)
Weight (empty): 8 624 lb (3 920 kg)
**Performances**
Max. take-off weight: 13 354 lb (6 070 kg)
Max. speed: 715 mph (1 145 kph) at 9 840 feet (3 000 m)
Service ceiling: 21 650 ft (6 600 m)
Range: 1 287 miles (2 060 km) (with drop tanks)
**Armament**
One 37-mm Nudelman N-37 canon; two 23-mm Nudelman-Rikhter NR-23 cannon. Up to 1 100 lb (500 kg) of weapons (bombs, unguided rockets or drop tanks) on two wing pylons.

Opposite:
An Egyptian MiG-17 seen from the ground showing the special shape of the Fresco's wings, quite different from the MiG-15.

successful in the export markets.

In Poland the WSK-PZL complex obtained a licence to build the MiG-17 and the VK-1F engine in the middle of the fifties. Built at the Mielec factory which gave up production of the Lim-2 (MiG-15) to do so, the first **Lim-5** first flew in November 1956. 477 examples of this fighter were built, most of which were delivered to 'friendly' countries and especially the DDR (East Germany) which received more than a hundred. From 1959 onwards WSK-PZL also built 130 **Lim-5P**s (like the end of production Soviet MiG-17 PFs, i.e. with the second generation 'Izumrud 2' radar), of which some were in turn exported [5].

This version itself gave rise to several versions and variants specially designed in Poland and produced in limited numbers. First of all, the tactical reconnaissance **Lim-5R** (35 ex.) fitted with a camera housed in a ventral fairing situated just behind the fuselage separation line; the tactical fighter Lim-5M fitted with extra tanks (57 gall./260 l in all) fitted to the fuselage, and with double wheels on the main undercarriage legs to allow it to operate from summarily prepared airstrips (60 ex., built in 1960-61; the survivors were transformed into Lim-6bis in 1964-65).

The **Lim-6** was in fact a Lim-5M (indeed its original designation was Lim-5M-II) equipped with blown flaps (the air coming from the engine) to improve take off and landing; its brake chute had been moved from under the exhaust nozzle to the base of the tailfin in a fairing. Forty examples of this version were built in 1961 but none was delivered to an operational unit, mainly because there were serious technical problems, like the engine suddenly cutting out.

The **Lim-6bis** was a sort of synthesis of the Lim-5M and the Lim-6 with their individual features (fuselage tanks, double wheel main undercarriage, blown flaps) removed; it only conserved the new housing for the brake chute, and two pylons for extra loads were added near the wing roots. A limited number of the Lim-6bis was produced (70 ex.) in 1963 and 1964 and gave rise to a tactical reconnaissance variant, the Lim-6R which carried a single AFA-39 camera housed in the same way as on the Lim-5R, in a ventral fairing.

In all more than 11 000 MiG-17s were built in all its versions including

Impeccable line-up of J-5s, the version of the MiG-17 produced in China, at the Shenyang factory. The machines in the foreground bear the "chung" ideogram in front of their code, indicating that they are pre-production series machines.

Above:
The MiG-17 turned out to be a formidable adversary for the Americans in the Vietnam War. Here North Vietnamese pilots returning from a mission.

under licence up to 1958 and although the type was withdrawn from service in the USSR at the end of the sixties, it was very successful abroad, the Fresco being the most exported Soviet fighter until the arrival of its indirect successor, the MiG-21.

---

5. At the beginning of the seventies, 40 Lim-5Ps were modified into fighter bombers under the designation Lim-6M. This modification consisted of suppressing the radars (but not the radomes) and adding two extra pylons (as on the standard Lim-6bis which could carry rocket panniers or bombs). In 1974 a further 14 Lim-5Ps were also transformed into tactical reconnaissance Lim-6MRs, the same as the standard Lim-6Ms but with the Lim-6R's photographic equipment.

# AFGHANISTAN

The Soviet Union delivered its first three MiG-15UTIs to the *Afghan Hanai Qurah*, the Democratic Republic of Afghanistan Air Force. These machines were in fact intended for training the pilots of the MiG-17F Frescoes that had been delivered to the country the same year. From 1960 until the eighties the Afghan Air Force possessed a fleet of about a hundred combat aircraft comprising mainly MiG-15s and 17s that were assigned to the 393rd Fighter-Bomber Regiment whose main base was situated at Mazar-a-Sharif in the northeast of the country. Following the revolution which took place in April 1978, the new government signed a treaty with the Soviet Union in December 1978 and during the civil war which obliged the Soviet Union to intervene in Afghanistan in December 1979 against the Mujahedin, the MiG-17 became the main combat aircraft used operationally by the country.

In the 1980s and at the beginning of the 1990s, the Afghan Air Force was at the height of its power since it had some 240 combat aircraft including fighters, fighter-bombers and light bombers, together with a hundred or so helicopters and forty-odd transport planes. The Afghan MiG-15UTIs seem to have remained operational until 1991 when more than thirty MiG-17Fs were still in service in the country.

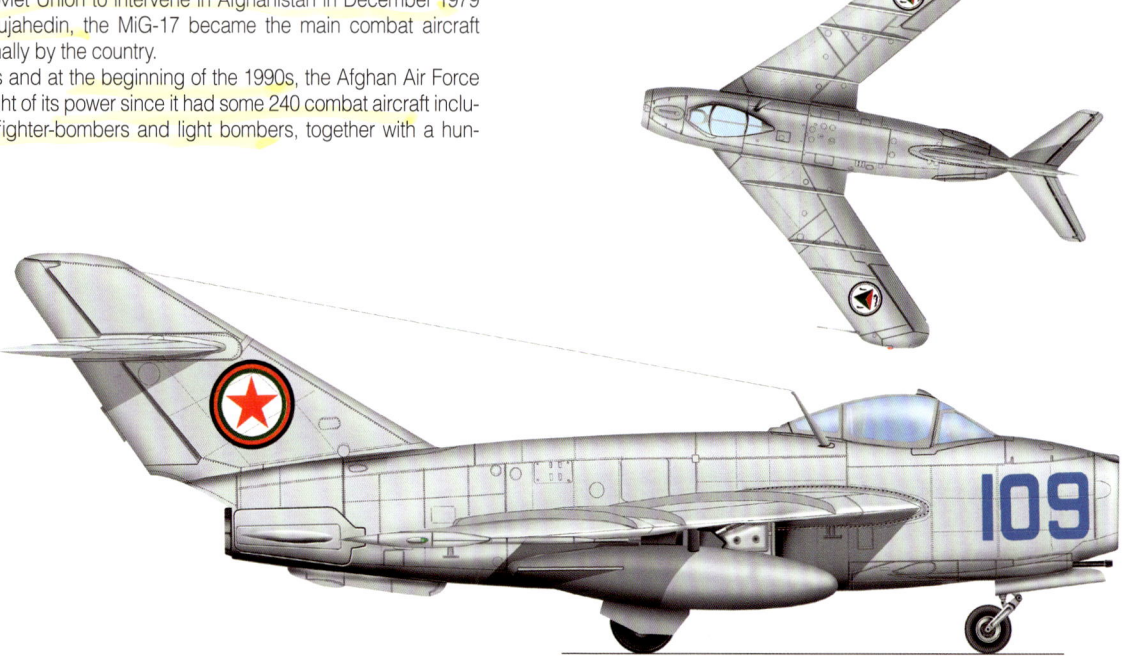

MiG-17 from the 335th Squadron of the *Afghan Hanai Qurah* (Afghan Air Force), Kandahar, 1982.

MiG-17F from the 335th Squadron of the Afghan Air Force, Kandahar, 1982.

MiG-17 from the 335th Squadron of the Afghan Air Force, Kandahar, 1979.

MiG-17F from an undetermined Afghan Air Force unit, 1980. This type of roundel was worn between 1980 and 1983.

# ALBANIA

Because of the Cold War, the development of the People's Republic of Albania's Air Force, the *Forçat Ajrore Shgipëtarë* (FASH), started as early as 1947 and intensified, ending in January 1955 with the first MiG-15bis and MiG-15UTI deliveries from the USSR. Two squadrons of MiG-15s thus constituted the 5818th Regiment based at Valona.

In 1962 relations with the Soviet Union were broken off and the country had therefore to turn to China for spare parts for its MiG-15bis, but also for its Shenyang F-2 (the Chinese-built version of the MiG-15bis) and FT-2s (MiG-15UTI), two types of machines delivered to Albania after 1956. The MiG-15bis were increasingly used as fighter-bombers but more than 25 of them were still operational in 1995 in the 5818th regiment at Valona. Twelve Midgets, of which four Soviet-built MiG-15UTIs, four Czech-built Aero-CS-102 built and four Shenyang FT-2s were apparently assigned to the 1875th Regiment based at Kuçova,

**MiG-15 from the 5818th Fighter Regiment of the *Forçat Ajrore Shgipëtarë* (FASH – Albanian Air Force), Valona, beginning of the 1950s.**

15

to the 5818th Regiment at Valona and the 7594th Regiment at Rinas respectively.

After 2000 most of the surviving MiG-15s were stocked on the bases at Kuçova and Rinas.

## MiG-17

A first contingent of ten MiG-17s Fresco As was delivered by the USSR to Albania in the middle of the fifties and after diplomatic relations between the two countries were broken off, China delivered ten or so Shenyang F-5s and a number of F-5As (MiG-17PF) all-weather interceptors in 1965. The air force appears to have comprised 23 Soviet MiG-17Fs, twelve Shenyang F-5s and twelve Shenyang F-5As in the 1875th Regiment based at Kuçova in 1995. To ensure the transition went smoothly between the MiG-15UTI and the MiG-19, Albania apparently purchased more than 30 Shenyang FT-5 advanced trainers.

All fixed-wing aircraft including the Soviet-and Chinese-built single-seat and two-seat MiG-17s were withdrawn from service at the end of 2004.

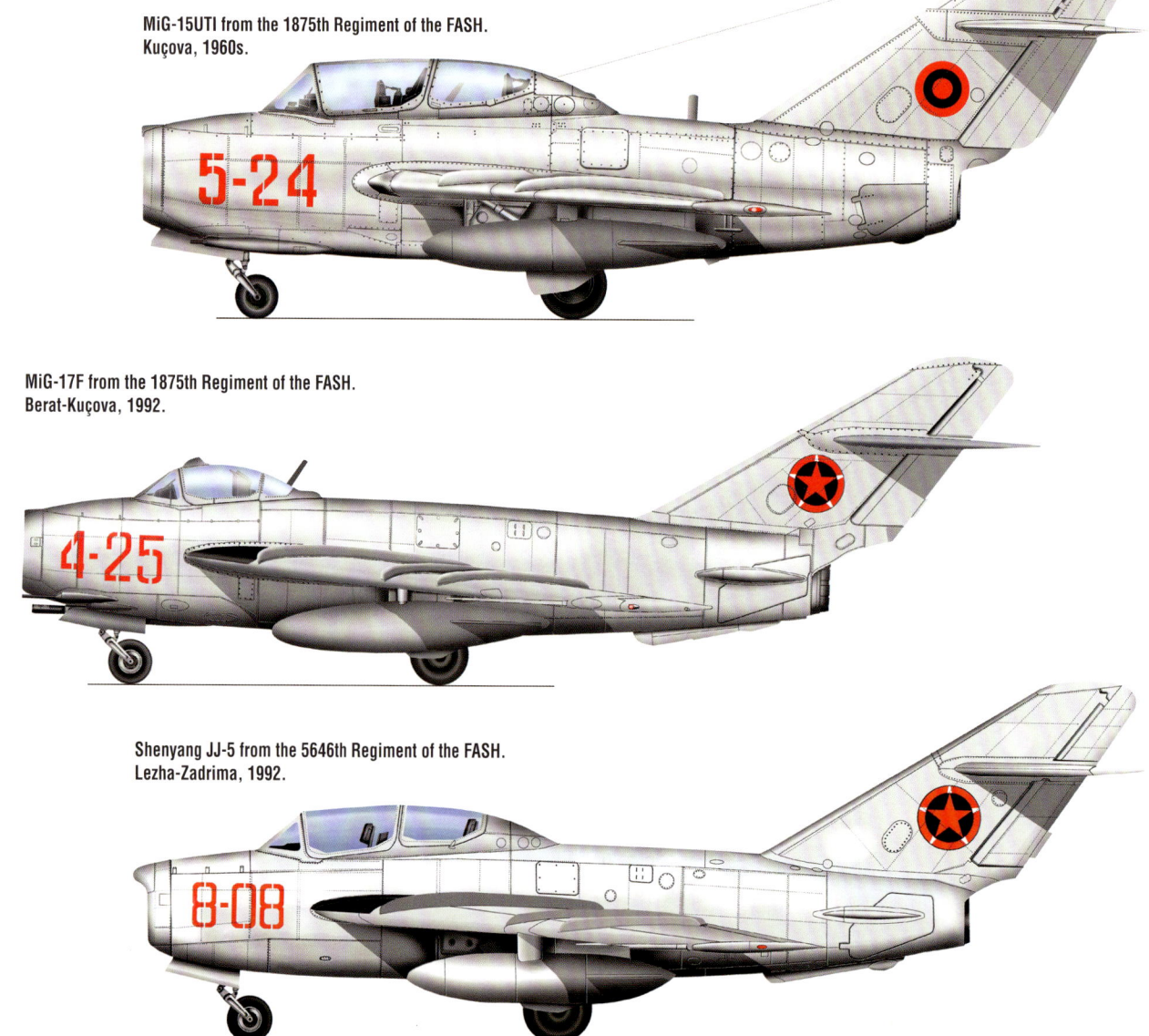

MiG-15UTI from the 1875th Regiment of the FASH. Kuçova, 1960s.

MiG-17F from the 1875th Regiment of the FASH. Berat-Kuçova, 1992.

Shenyang JJ-5 from the 5646th Regiment of the FASH. Lezha-Zadrima, 1992.

# ALGERIA

Created in 1962, the Algerian Air Force (after 1965 the *Al-Quwwat al-Jawwiya al-Jaza'iriya*) sent a first group of pilots to the Middle East for training and at the same time received twenty or so Egyptian-built trainers as well as a number of MiG-15s.

In 1964, Algeria received its first Soviet-built aircraft together with the benefit of East European bloc experts and logistics. Following the 'Sand War' against Morocco in 1963, Algeria set up a large training and armament programme and received its first attack aircraft in the form of fifty-odd MiG-15bis and MiG-17Fs.

In 1965 another modernisation programme was organised with the Soviet Union. Algeria then purchased its first modern combat aircraft, some MiG-17Fs that were assigned to two fighter-bomber squadrons.

It was in 1967, during the Six Days War, that the Algerian pilots had their baptism of fire when four squadrons participated in the Arab coalition against Israel: two of MiG-17Fs, one of MiG-21s and one of Il-28 'Beagle' bombers.

At the beginning of 1971, the Algerian Air Force numbered some 200 machines of different types and Sukhoi Su-7BMK fighter-bombers started to replace the MiG-17Fs. In 1973 During the Yom Kippur War, Algeria engaged a squadron of Su-7s escorted by a MiG-21 fighter squadron with a squadron of MiG-17s sent as back up.

At the beginning of 1978, Algeria had 230 combat aircraft of which several MiG-15s and MiG-17Fs, planes that have now been withdrawn from service once and for all.

MiG-15bis of the l'*Al Quwwat al Jawwiya al Jaza'iriya* (Algerian Air Force), 1964-65.

CS-102 from the Algerian Air Force, 1984.

MiG-17F from the 19th Squadron from the Algerian Air Force, June 1967.

# ANGOLA

After Angola won its independence in November 1975, civil war tore the country apart with three political movements struggling to take power: the UNITA (*União Nacional para a Independência Total de Angola*), supported by the United States and South Africa, the pro-Zaire FNLA (*Frente Nacional de Libertação de Angola*), and the MPLA (*Movimento Popular de Libertação de Angola*), in power at the time and backed by the Eastern bloc and Cuba.

When it was besieged the MPLA turned to Cuba for help in setting up the *Força Aérea Nacional Angolana* (FANA, the Angolan Air Force) which was created in January 1976 under the name of *Força Aérea Popular de Angola/Defesa Aérea e Antiaérea* (FAPA/DAA). The Cubans supplied them with their first MiG-15 UTIS and ten or so MiG-17Fs and these were used in the fighting which took place in the north and the centre of the country from 1975 onwards until the eighties.

In all, the Angolan Air Force received fifty or so MiG-15s and MiG-17Fs that used several air bases including Luanda and Lubango. The MiG-15UTIs were withdrawn from service in the middle of the eighties and the MiG-17Fs in 1999.

MiG-15UTI of the *Força Aérea Popular de Angola* (FAPA), 1976.

MiG-17F 'Fresco C' of the FAPA, Luanda, 1976.

MiG-17F 'Fresco C' of the FAPA, Luanda, 1976.

# BANGLADESH

The *Bangladesh Biman Bahini*, the Bangladesh Air Force, created in September 1971 after it separated from Pakistan, received some Shenyang FT-5s, the export version of the Chengdu JJ-5, itself based on the MiG-17PF; these were based at Tejgaon (Bashar), the former international airport of the capital, Dacca.

Shenyang FT-5 of the *Bangladesh Biman Bahini* (Bangladesh Air Force). Tejgaon, 1976.

# BULGARIA

## MiG-15

After the Second World War, the *Bulgarski Voenno Vzdushni Sili* (BVVS – Bulgarian Air Force) started to equip with jet fighters, some Yak-23s, which were replaced in 1952 by MiG-15s, MiG-15bis and MiG-15UTIs.

The Soviet Union and Czechoslovakia delivered a hundred or so planes enabling two fighter regiments to be equipped, one based at Graf Ignatievo and the other at Tobulkhin (later renamed Dobrich). Moreover an independent reconnaissance regiment also based at Tolbulkhin and comprising a squadron of MiG-15bisR was set up as early as 1960.

With the appearance of more modern machines (MiG-19S and MiG-21), the Bulgarian MiG-15s were transferred to the fighter-bomber units so that in the middle of the 1980s there were only some MiG-15UTIs still operational in Bulgaria. In the 1990s fifteen or so of these machines were used by the Bulgarian Air Force training centre at its base at Dolna Mitropolia.

## MiG-17

From 1955 onwards MiG-17F 'Fresco C' and MiG-17PF 'Fresco D' started replacing the 'Fagot A' and B in the Bulgarian Air Force, these machines being used by six squadrons, joined by an independent reconnaissance regiment equipped with MiG-17Rs in 1963.

At the beginning of the sixties, MiG-19 Farmers started replacing the Frescoes which were therefore transferred to the ground attack units. However, the Farmers' unreliability and their high attrition rate meant that the MiG-17Fs and PFs had to return to service. The last Bulgarian MiG-17s were withdrawn from service in 1988 and replaced the same year by the Su-25 Frogfoot, given the ground attack and reconnaissance roles.

MiG-15 from the 19. IAP (*Iztrebitel Avio Polk* – Fighter Regiment) of the *Bulgarski Voenno Vzdushni Sili* (BVVS, Bulgarian Air Force), Graf Ignatievo, 1952.

MiG-15MT (UTI) from an unknown BVVS unit, Bulgaria, 1962.

MiG-17PF Fresco D from the 21. IAP in the 1970s.

MiG-17PF Fresco D from an undetermined BVVS unit in the 1980s. This machine is wearing non-standard camouflage.

MiG-17F Fresco C from the 19. IAP of the BVVS, Graf Ignatievo, end of the 1960s.

# BURKINA FASO

In 1964, the Burkina Faso (ex-Upper Volta) Air Force was set up under the name of '*Escadrille de République de Haute Volta*' (EHV).

Officially inaugurated in October 1985, it was then renamed '*Force Aérienne du Burkina Faso*' (FABF) and finally '*Armée de l'Air Burkinabé*' (AAB).

The FABF/AAB was equipped with a single MiG-17F based at Ouagadougou that was engaged in the 'Agacher Strip War' (or the 'Christmas War') against its neighbour, Mali, in December 1985. This plane – a wreck – was spotted in Burkina Faso at the beginning of the 2000s.

MiG-17F 'Fresco C' of the *Force Aérienne du Burkina Faso*. Ouagadougou, 1984.

# CAMBODIA

Created in April 1954 during Norodom Sihanouk's reign with French backing, the Royal Khmer Air Force (*Aviation Royale Khmère* or AVRK), started building up its own combat aircraft fleet. From 1955 to 1962, the AVRK received help from France, the United States and Israel, setting up training programmes and supplying technical back-up together with training, liaison, observation and transport aircraft. The Cambodian Air Force however could only ensure infantry unit transport and close quarters air support because it did not have the money.

The increasingly deteriorating situation in Vietnam made Cambodia buy helicopters and Fouga Magisters which were delivered in 1961. As early as 1960 however, the head of state, Norodom Sihanouk, had started getting closer to the Eastern bloc countries and a certain number of Cambodian pilots were sent to the Soviet Union to train on MiG-17s. After 1963, the first MiG-15UTIs and MiG-17Fs were delivered to Cambodia by the USSR. Norodom Sihanouk also turned to China which supplied some MiG-15UTIs and MiG-17s.

In March 1970, a military coup overthrew Norodom Sihanouk and at the time, the *Groupe Aérien Tactique de l'Aviation Royale Khmère* (renamed Armée de l'Air Khmère, or AAK, in 1971) had a fleet of 143 planes of different types bought off France, the United States, the USSR, China, Yugoslavia and Canada. These machines were shared out among four units including an advanced training squadron, an interception group comprising twelve MiG-17Fs, six Shenyang J-5s and one MiG-15UTI, a combat observation group, a transport and liaison group and finally a helicopter group.

Other machines joined this fleet between 1962 and 1966, either handed over by various countries or flown there by deserting VNAF pilots. Most of the aircraft were destroyed in January 1970 during an air raid carried out against two air bases located near Phnom-Penh including the one at Pochentong by the *Front National de Libération du Sud-Vietnam* (FNL) – the Vietcong,

The aircraft that survived the raid were incorporated into a unit of bombers in June 1971 but they were quickly withdrawn from service because there were no spare parts for servicing.

**Shenyang FT-2 from the *Aviation Royale Khmère* (AVRK- Royal Khmer Air Force), Cambodia 1967.**

**AVRK Shenyang FT-2, Cambodia, 1970s.**

23

AVRK MiG-17F 'Fresco C', Cambodia, 1970s. The Cambodian MiG-17F had a medium grey-blue livery.

Armée de l'Air Khmère (AAK) MiG-17F 'Fresco C' Cambodia, 1972.

# CHINA (People's Republic of China/PRC)

## MiG-15

It was in 1950 that the first training jets —Yak-17UTIs— together with MiG-9 fighters were delivered to China by the USSR. In the same year a Soviet Air Force unit equipped with 40 MiG-15s was deployed in the country to back up the new *Zhongguó Rénmín Jiefàngjun Kongjun* – the People's Liberation Army's Air force/PLAAF – especially to make sure the nation's new capital, Peking, was protected against possible air raids by the Nationalist China's Air Force under Tchang Kai Chek (Taiwan).

MiG-15bis of the People's Liberation Army Air Force (PLAAF) – the *Zhongguó Renmín Jiefangjun Kongjun*, 1951.

MiG-15 from the 151. GvIAD (151st Air Division of the Guard), 72. GvIAP (72nd Air Regiment of the Guard) of the VVS (Soviet Air Force). Ansan (Korea), November 1950. Pilot: Major Nikolay V. Stoykov.

When the Korean War broke out in June 1950, most of the Soviet MiG-15s deployed in China were handed over to China, whilst the Soviet Air Force detachment was sent to Korea. The Chinese pilots who trained on MiG-15s in the USSR were however only operational in the spring of 1951.

More than 650 MiG-15s were delivered between October 1950 and 1951 followed by a further 1500-odd MiG-15bis between 1952 and 1955, planes which were renamed J-2 by the Chinese.

The USSR and Czechoslovakia delivered more than 350 MiG-15UTIs between 1951 and 1958. This two-seater was also licence-built in China in the aircraft factory at Shenyang from 1956 onwards using the name Shenyang JJ-2.

The *Zhongguó Rénmín Jiefàngjun Haijun*, the People's Liberation Army's Navy Air Force also used MiG-15bis and JJ-2s.

When the MiG-17F (built under licence in China under the name of Shenyang JJ-2) became China's main tactical fighter in the sixties, all the MiG15bis (J-2s) were converted to fighter-bombers. A certain number of these machines were sold for export and in the middle of the 1980s, there were still about a hundred J-2s and three times more JJ-2s still serving in the People's Republic of China.

## MiG-17

Several Air Force and Navy Air Force regiments received Shenyang J-5s (licence-built MiG-17Fs) and took part in the various clashes with Nationalist China (Taiwan) from 1956 to 1960 when they faced F-100 Super Sabres, F-101/RF-101 Voodoos and Lockheed F-104 Starfighters, along with ROCAF (the Taiwanese Air Force) F-86Fs.

The J-5 and the JJ-5 (the two-seat training version built in China) were used a lot by the PRC, especially by its Navy Air Force until they were replaced by the new generation of fighters. A national acrobatic team called the 'August First' was formed in 1962 and equipped with nine red and white Shenyang JJ-5s.

MiG-15 from the People's Liberation Army Air Force during the Korean War.

Shenyang JJ-2 from an undetermined People's Liberation Army Air Force unit.

MiG-15bis from the PLAAF in the 1950s.

Shenyang J-5 of the 38th Air Division of the PLAAF. Yang Tsuon, 1980.

Chengdu JJ-5 from the Pilots School of the 38th Air Division of the PLAAF. Shijiazhuang, 1980.

Chengdu JJ-5 of the 38th Air Division of the PLAAF. 'August First' aerobatic team. Yang Tsuon, 1980.

Shenyang J-5 of the PLAAF in the 1970's.

Chengdu J-5A from the PLAAF in the 1960-70s.

27

# CONGO-BRAZZAVILLE

The Congolese Air Force started to equip with Soviet-built combat aircraft during the seventies and at the end of 1991 it had ten or so MiG-17 Fresco As in a single fighter flight, together with a few MiG-15UTIs for pilot training. In the same year, all these machines were withdrawn from service and stored at Agostinho-Neto airport, at Pointe-Noire.

**Aero CS-102 from the *Armée de l'Air du Congo* (Congo Air Force). 1991.**

**MiG-17 Fresco A from the *Escadrille de Chasse* (Fighter Flight) of the *Armée de l'Air du Congo*, Air Base 02/20. Pointe Noire, 1997.**

# CUBA

## MiG-15

When Fidel Castro took power in February 1959 following the revolution started in 1953 and ending with the overthrow of the pro-American dictator, Fulgencio Batista, the USSR started delivering combat planes to Cuba, especially MiG-15s. These fighters were used to form the new *Fuerza Aérea Revolucionaria* (FAR – the Cuban Air Force) and were grouped together on the air base at San Antonio de Los Banos with a reconnaissance squadron based at Ciudad Libertad.

By the end of 1961, 41 MiG-15bis Fagot Bs, including the recce (MiG-15Rbis) and the two-seat trainer (MiG-15UTI) variants had been delivered to the Caribbean island. The following year the USSR supplied a further 30 MiG-15bis, as well as more MiG-15UTIs for training future MiG-17 and MiG-19 pilots.

At the end of 1991, about ten MiG-15bis and fifteen or so MiG-15 UTIs were still in service on the base at San Antonio de Los Banos and on other bases.

## MiG-17

The first MiG-17 Fresco As and MiG-17F Fresco Cs reached Cuba in 1964 with deliveries carrying on into 1971 so that in the end the FAR had received 75 MiG-17s by the beginning of the 1970s. These fighters were declassified when the more modern MiG-21s and MiG-23s arrived and were used as fighter-bombers in four squadrons, with a strength of about a hundred machines. The FAR used another twenty or so MiG-17s for ground attack until the end of 1991. The MiG-15s and MiG-17s were withdrawn from service once and for all in Cuba at the end of the nineties.

MiG-15bis of the *Fuerza Aérea Revolucionaria* (FAR, Cuban Air Force). Cuba, 1962.

MiG-15UTI of the FAR at the end of the eighties.

MiG-17 'Fresco A' of the FAR. It was aboard this machine that the *Tenente* (lieutenant) Eduardo Jimenez deserted and landed at Homestead AFB, Florida, on 5 October 1969.

29

MiG-15UTI of the FAR. San Antonio de Los Banos, 1962.

MiG-17F 'Fresco C' of the FAR. Cuba, 1974.

# CZECHOSLOVAKIA

## MiG-15

The MiG-15 had an important place in post-war Czechoslovakia since it was the main fighter and fighter-bomber strength in the Czech Air Force – the *Czeskoslovenské Vojenské Létectvo* – in the fifties and sixties.

In June 1951, 62 MiG-15 and four MiG-15UTI trainers were delivered to Czechoslovakia from the USSR, with construction under licence of the aircraft under the designation S-102 (MiG-15 Fagot A) beginning at the end of the same year. This was followed in 1954 by production of the S-103 (MiG-15bis 'Fagot B') and the CS-102 (MiG-15UTI 'Midget'). From then on the Czech Air Force was equipped only with Czech-built aircraft.

At the end of 1957 about 1 200 MiG-15s were in service in eighteen fighter units, two reconnaissance units and two operational conversion units, whilst others were shared out among several other smaller units.

From 1958 onwards, rearmament and reorganisation programmes were started in Czechoslovakia and the MiG-15s were converted into MiG-15SB fighter-bombers whilst the MiG-15bis were themselves modernised and renamed MiG-15bisSB.

In 1964 these machines were joined by Sukhoi Su-7 'Fitter' As but the Czech MiG-15SBs and MiG-15bisSBs remained in service until 1966 and 1983 respectively, or thirty-two years. As for the MiG-15UTIs, they remained in service in the fighter units until 1984.

## MiG-17

Czechoslovakia was one of the first foreign countries to receive MiG-17s, but it did not use a lot of them since in the end its fleet only consisted of a few MiG-17F Fresco Cs and thirty-odd MiG-19PF Fresco Ds which entered service in 1955. This model designated locally as the S-104 was equipped with radar and was built in Tbilissi, in Georgia. Czechoslovakia which also owned a lot of MiG-19Ss, MiG-19Ps and

MiG-19PMs thought it wiser however to licence-build the supersonic MiG-19S (local designation S-105) which then went on to become the mainstay of its supersonic fighter fleet until it was replaced by the MiG-21F-13 (built under licence as the S-107).

The MiG-17 remained operational in the Czech Air Force for fourteen years and was withdrawn from service in 1969.

Aero S-103 of the *Ceskoslovenské Vojenske Letectvo* (Czech Air Force) Acrobatic Team, 1957.

Czech Air Force Aero S-103 at the beginning of the sixties.

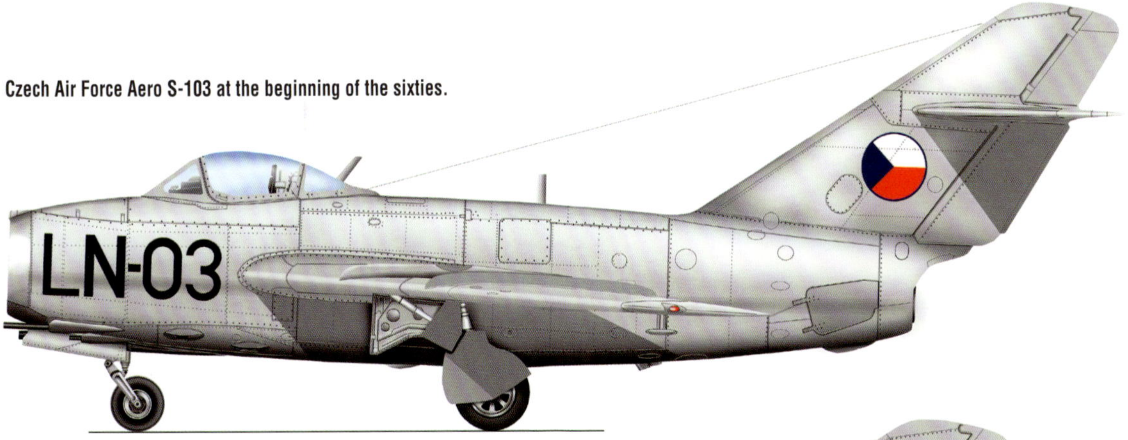

Czech Air Force Aero S-102. Special markings used during exercises in the 1950s.

31

Czech Air Force Aero S-103. Special markings used during manoeuvres in the 1960s.

Czech Air Force Aero S-102. This machine bears special markings used for air combat training at the beginning of the sixties.

Aero CS-102 from the 30. SBoLP (*Stihaci Bombardovaci Letecky Pulk* – 30th Fighter-Bomber Regiment). Malacky, 1982.

Aero S-103 from the Divisional Command Flight. This was the personal mount of the Divisional Chief of Operations. České Budejovice-Plan, March 1956.

Aero S-104 from the 11. SLP/1. Zatec, 1957.

# EGYPT

## MiG-15

After the Egyptian revolution in July 1952 started by the Free Officers Movement led by Mohammed Naguib and Gamal Abdel Nasser which abolished the monarchy, the Egyptian government turned to Czechoslovakia to get hold of weapons, in particular planes for its air force (the *Al Quwwat al-Jawwiya il-Misriya*).

In October 1955, more than a hundred Aero S-103s (Czech-built MiG-15bis) were delivered and the following year sixty-odd of these machines were in service in six squadrons (Nos 15, 18, 20, 24 and 30) based mainly at El Qabrit, Abu Suair and Inshas. Most of the Egyptian MiG-15s did not take part however in the fighting during the Suez Crisis, from October 1956 to March 1957.

After 1956, most fighter deliveries consisted of MiG-17Fs and MiG-19s as well as Aero CS-102 two seat trainers. During the Six Day War, from 5 to 10 June 1967, the last surviving Egyptian MiG-15s were destroyed on the ground by Israeli aircraft.

## MiG-17

In the autumn of 1956 the first Soviet-built MiG-17F Fresco Cs were delivered to Egypt to reinforce its air force, at a time of heavy tension with Israel, France and the United Kingdom in the Suez Canal Zone. The jets took part in the conflict from their base at El Qabrit. In June 1957, three months after French and British troops withdrew from the Suez Canal Zone, the Egyptian Air Force had more than one hundred MiG-17Fs based at Almaza, near Cairo.

At the beginning of the 1960s, after the delivery of MiG-19Ss and MiG-21F-13s, the United Arab Republic (of which Egypt was part, alongside Syria) MiG-17Fs were relegated to ground attack.

During the Yom Kippur War (6-25 October 1973), the Egyptian MiG-17Fs were used mainly against ground targets and their effectiveness was such that they remained in service until 1987.

**MiG-15bis of the *Al Qwwat al-Jawwiya il-Misriya* (Egyptian Air Force) in 1956, at the time of the Suez Crisis. The black wing and fuselage stripes were rapid identification markings worn by all Egyptian fighters after 1948.**

**Aero S-103 of the No 18 Squadron, 1958.**

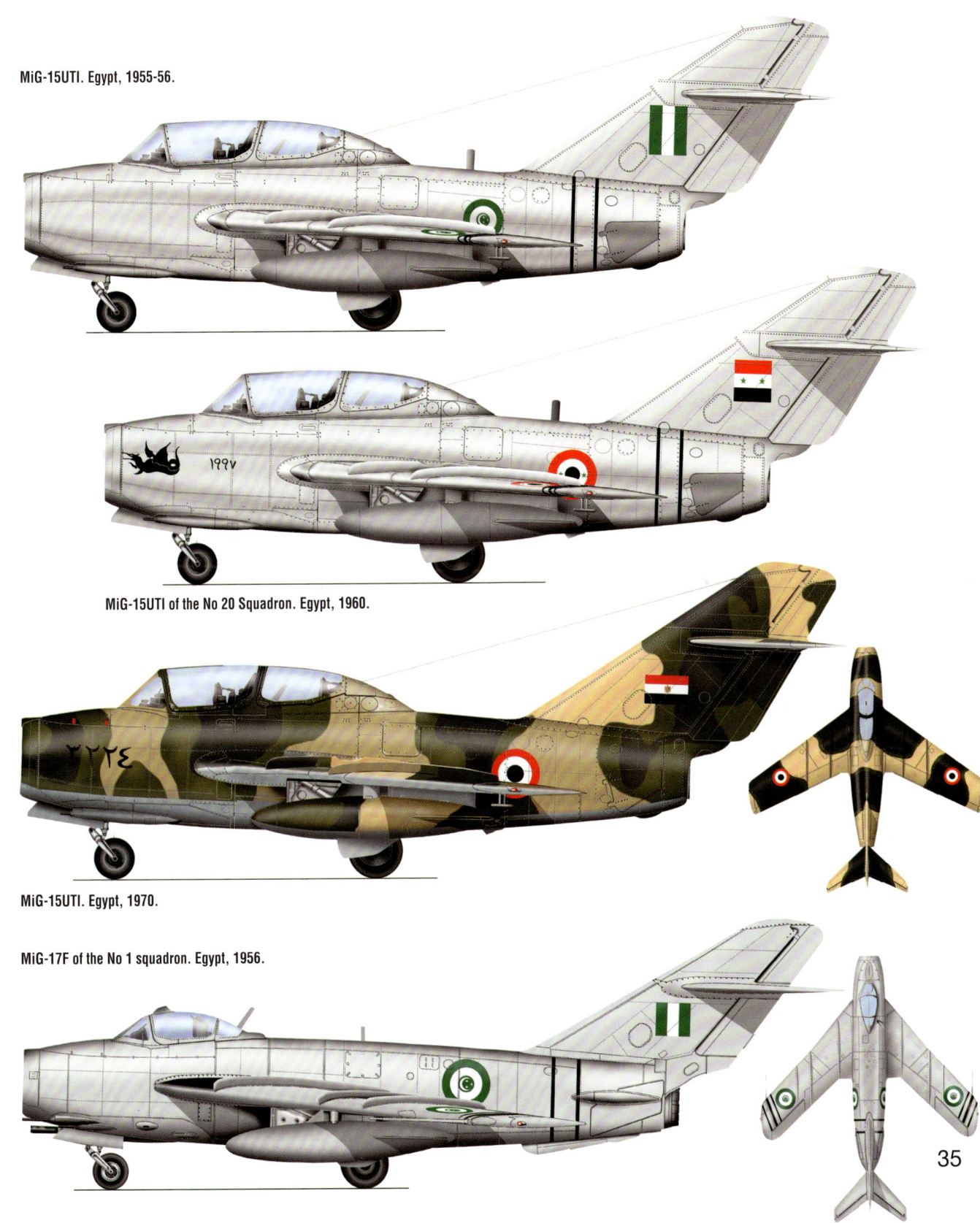

MiG-17F from No 18 Squadron of the Egyptian Air Force (EAF), June 1967.

MiG-17PF 'Fresco D' from No 31 Squadron of the EAF, June 1967.

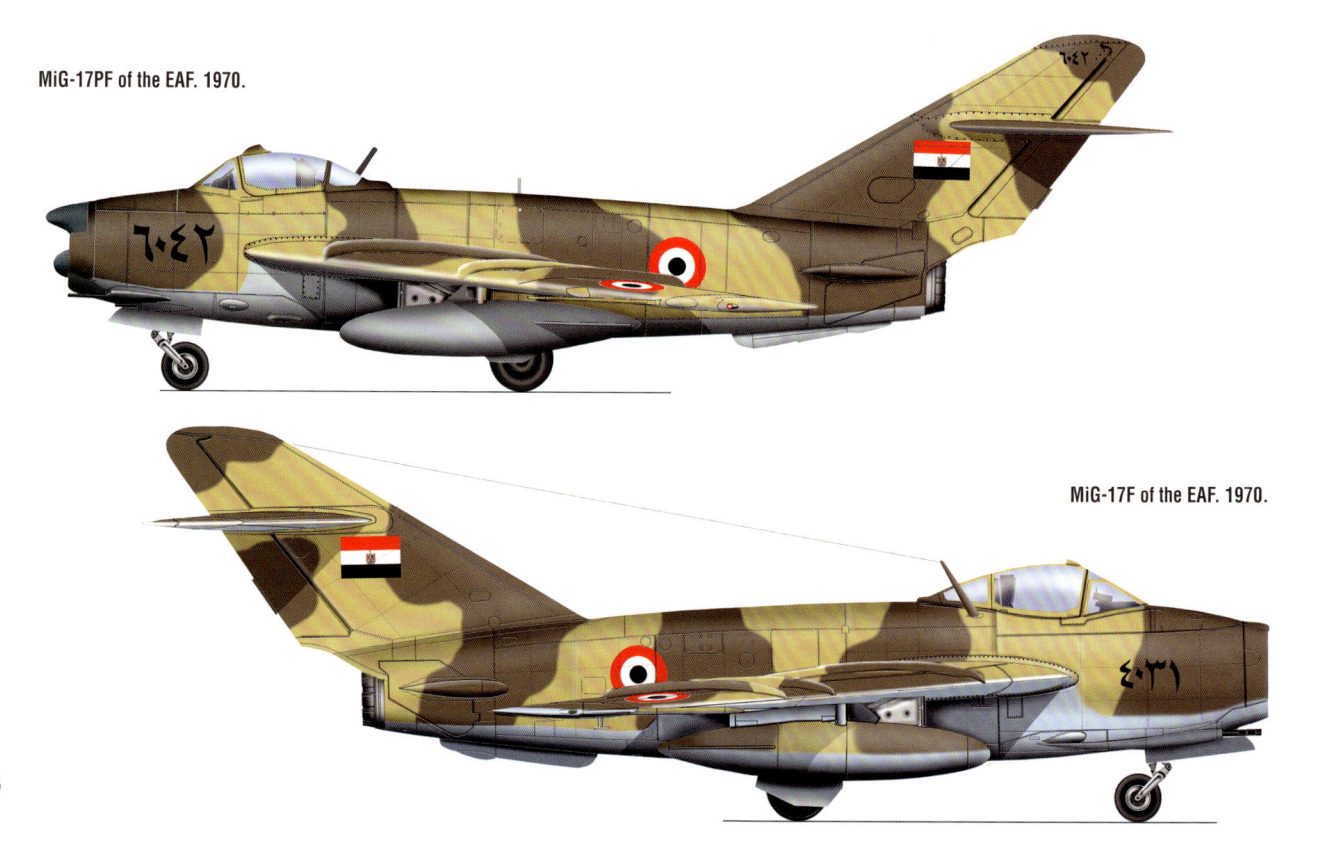

MiG-17PF of the EAF. 1970.

MiG-17F of the EAF. 1970.

MiG-17F of the Egyptian Air Force in 1973. This camouflage scheme, called the 'Nile Delta' was worn by the MiG-17Fs and differed from one machine to another.

# FINLAND

As part of its Cold War neutrality and non-alignment policy, Finland turned both to the East and to the West to purchase its military equipment. Thus in 1962, the Suomen Ilmavoimat (Finnish Air Force) received four latest generation Czech-built Aero CS-102s (MiG-15UTIs). These planes were used by a single fighter unit, the HävLv 31 (*Hävittäjälentolaivue 31*—31st Fighter Squadron), based at Kuopio-Rissala. The Midgets remained in service until 1978 when they were replaced by the MiG-21UM Mongol.

MiG-15-UTI from the HävLv 31 of the *Suomen Ilmavoimat* (Finnish Air Force). Keväällä, 1963.

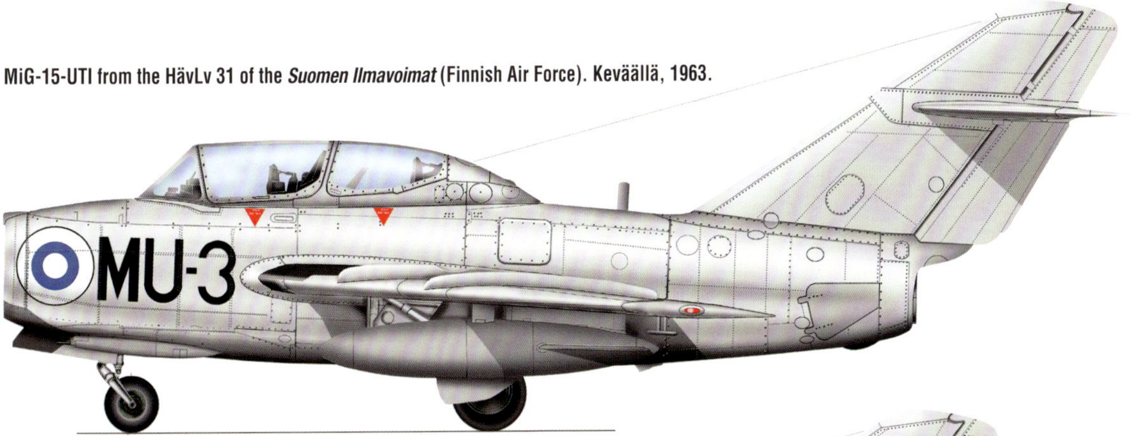

MiG-15-UTI from the HävLv 31 of the *Suomen Ilmavoimat*. Keväällä, 1971.

# EAST GERMANY (German Democratic Republic)

## MiG-15

On 1 March 1956 the *Luftstreitkräfte und Luftverteidigung der Deutschen Demokratischen Republik* (LSK/LV, the German Democratic Republic Air Force and Air Defence Force) was set up shortly after the creation of the *Nationale Volksarmee* (NVA- People's National Army) a few months earlier following East Germany's joining the Warsaw pact in May 1955. Several years earlier however in September 1951 nearly 300 East German pilots along with technical staff had started training on MiG-15s in the Soviet Union. This training was continued directly in East Germany on the base at Cottbus as of August 1952.

In April 1953, more than a hundred MiG-15s were loaned by the Soviet Union to the East German Air Force (which at the time was still called the *Kasernierte Volkspolizei-Luft*—KVP-Luft—Popular Air Police), but the training was interrupted the following June because of an anti-communist uprising and all the planes came back under Soviet Control.

In the summer of 1956, the first air group of the LSK/LV, the Fliegergeschwader-1 (FG-1) settled at Cottbus and replaced its propeller-driven Yak-11s and Yak-18s with jet planes. On this occasion the unit received its first MiG-15bis and MiG-15 UTIs, in this case Aero S-103s and CS-102s built under licence in Czechoslovakia. In all thirty S-103s were delivered to the LSK/LV, as well as some second-hand MiG-15Bbis and more than 140 Midgets mainly coming from Czechoslovakia.

Conversion to the MiG-15 started for the FG-1 in January 1957 with fifteen or so planes but in September of the same year, the unit had already started to re-equip with MiG-17Fs and soon there were no more MiG-15s left in its ranks.

The group changed its name twice at the beginning of 1961 because at first it was called JFG-1 (*Jagdfliegergeschwader-1* – 1st Fighter Group) then JG-1 (*Jagdgeschwader-1*).

The MiG-15 was used by five East German fighter groups during the period 1956-59:
- FG-2 (the JFG-2 then finally JG-2), based at Trollenhagen (Mecklenburg-Western Pomerania), from 1956 to 1957.
- FG-3 (JFG-3, JG-3) based at Preschen (Brandenburg) from 1956 to 1959.
- FG-7 (JFG-7, JG-7) based at Drewitz (Brandenburg) from 1956 to 1959.
- FG-8 (JFG-8, JG-8) based at Marxwalde (Brandenburg) in 1957.
- FG-9 (JFG-9, JG-9) based at Drewitz (Brandenburg) from 1956 to 1957.

A certain number of machines also served in four training units:
- FAG-2 (*Fliegerausbildungsgeschwader-2*, subsequently FAG-25) based initially at Bautzen (Saxony), which flew MiG-15bis from 1958 to 1965.
- FAG-3 (the FAG-15) based at Bautzen, equipped with MiG-15bis from 1959 to 1964.
- JAG-11 (*Jagdfliegerausbildungsgeschwader-11*).
- JAS-23 (*Jagdfliegerausbildungsstaffel-23*).

FG-1 (JFG-1, JG-1) used MiG-15UTIs until the middle of the sixties for the pilots' operational qualification, with the Midget also being used in the sixties and seventies by the FG-2, FG7, FG-8, FG-9, FAG-15, FAG-25 and the JBG-31 (*Jagdbombenfliegergeschwader-31*, 31st Fighter-Bomber Group) based at Drewitz during the seventies.

As well as their air defence role, the MiG-15s were also used for close support, attack and reconnaissance. Withdrawal of the MiG-15bis began at the end of the fifties, when it was replaced by the MiG-17, but the MiG-15UTI remained in service until the end of the seventies.

## MiG-17

The MiG-17F Fresco Cs entered service in the LSK/LV during the summer of 1957, most of them being in fact licence-built Polish Lim-5s. More than a hundred of these fighters were put into service between 1957 and 1968 in six fighter groups including:

JFG-1 (JG-1) at Cottbus,

Aero S-103 from an unidentified unit of the *Luftstreitkräfte und Luftverteidigung der Deutschen Demokratischen Republik* (LSK/LV—the German Democratic Republic Air and Defence Force) 1956. This type of roundel dated back to an earlier period.

FG-2 (JFG-2, JG-2) at Trollenhagen,
FG-3 (JFG-3, JG-3) at Preschen,
FG-7 (JFG-7, JG-7) at Drewitz,
FG-8 (JFG-8, JG-8) at Marxwalde,
FG-9 (JFG-9, JG-9) at Drewitz.

More than 120 MiG-17 Fresco As were delivered to JV-1, JG-2 and JG-7 as well as to training units from 1960 and 1966. From 1959 onwards, forty or so Polish-built Lim-5Ps (MiG-17PFs) were delivered to the LSK/LV and put into service in the JG-1, JG-2, JG-7 and JG-9, these machines being capable of both day and night all-weather interception. The arrival of the MiG-21 in East Germany relegated the MiG-17F to the role of fighter-bomber, this type being especially assigned to the JBG-51 at Drewitz which at the end of 1971 had a fleet of forty or so examples, holding on to them until 1983. On the other hand the MiG-17 Fresco As and the Lim-5Ps were withdrawn from service.

**Aero S-103 from an unidentified LSK/LV unit at the beginning of the 1960s. This type of roundel was worn after 1959.**

**Aero CS-102 from an unidentified LSK/LV unit in 1976.**

**Aero CS-102 from an unidentified LSK/LV unit in the 1980s.**

39

MiG-17 'Fresco A' from the JG-1 of the LSK/LV, 1960.

MiG-17F 'Fresco C' from an unidentified LSK/LV unit. This roundel was worn between 1956 and 1959.

MiG-17F from the Jagdfliegergeschwader-7. Drewitz, 1980s.

**MiG-17PF 'Fresco D' from an unidentified LSK/LV unit in 1964.**

**MiG-17PF 'Fresco D' from an unidentified LSK/LV unit in the 1970s.**

41

# GUINEA-BISSAU

Set up at the beginning of the seventies before the country's independence was proclaimed in September 1974, the Guinea-Bissau Air Force (which later took the name of *Força Aérea da Guinée-Bissau* or FAGB) obtained East German and Soviet backing. It made up an air force consisting of two MiG-15UTIs and five MiG-17F Fresco Cs based at the airport at Bissau (formerly Bissalanca).

The end of the Cold War in 1991 put an end to the technical support given by the Eastern bloc and the jets still in service were stored in some of the Bissau Airport hangars.

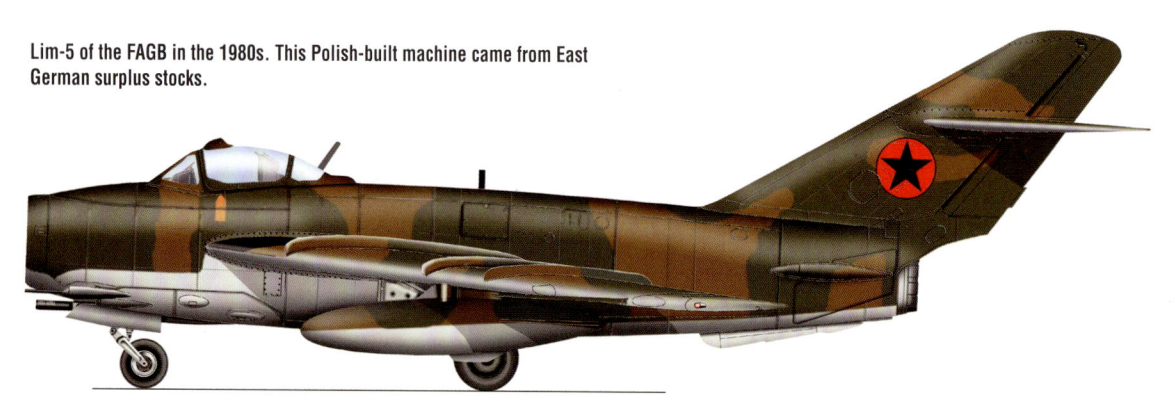

MiG-15UTI of the *Força Aérea da Guinée-Bissau* (FAGB). Bissalanca, 1985.

MiG-17F 'Fresco C' of the FAGB in 1991.

Lim-5 of the FAGB in the 1980s. This Polish-built machine came from East German surplus stocks.

# GUINEA-CONAKRY

After Guinea became independent in 1958, the *Force Aérienne de Guinée* (the Guinea Air Force) received support from the USSR with the delivery of ten or so MiG-17F Fresco Cs and two MiG-15UTI trainers that were all based at Conakry. When the Russians obtained Guinean government permission to use Conakry airport for their Navy aircraft, in return the *Force Aérienne de Guinée* received some MiG-21PFMs as well as a MiG-21U in 1986 to replace its Frescoes still in service. There were however several MiG-17Fs which were still in service until the beginning of the eighties, with the MiG-15UTIs being withdrawn from service in 1982.

**Force Aérienne de Guinée MiG-17 'Fresco A' at the end of the 1960s.**

# HUNGARY

At the beginning of the fifties, Hungary was one of the first Warsaw Pact countries to receive Soviet-built MiG-15s. After 1953, both Soviet- and Czech-built MiG-15bis and MiG-15UTIs were delivered to the country, the first consignment of Fagots being sent back to the Soviet Union. At the time of the anti-communist uprising in 1956 and the subsequent Soviet repression, the *Magyar Honvedseg Repülö Csapatai* (the Hungarian Air Force) was reduced so that in 1958 there remained only three squadrons of MiG-15s.

A certain number of MiG-15s were subsequently withdrawn from service and stored away and others were put on display in museums. Some MiG-15UTIs were still in service however during the nineties.

Deliveries of MiG-17F Fresco Cs and MiG17 PF Fresco Ds started in 1956, the planes being assigned to the 50th Fighter Regiment based at Taszar. These machines were replaced at the end of the sixties by MiG-19s.

**MiG-15bis from an unidentified *Magyar Honvedseg Repülö Csapatai* (MHRCS – Hungarian Air Force) unit in 1953. The squadron code (letter D) was worn on the fin.**

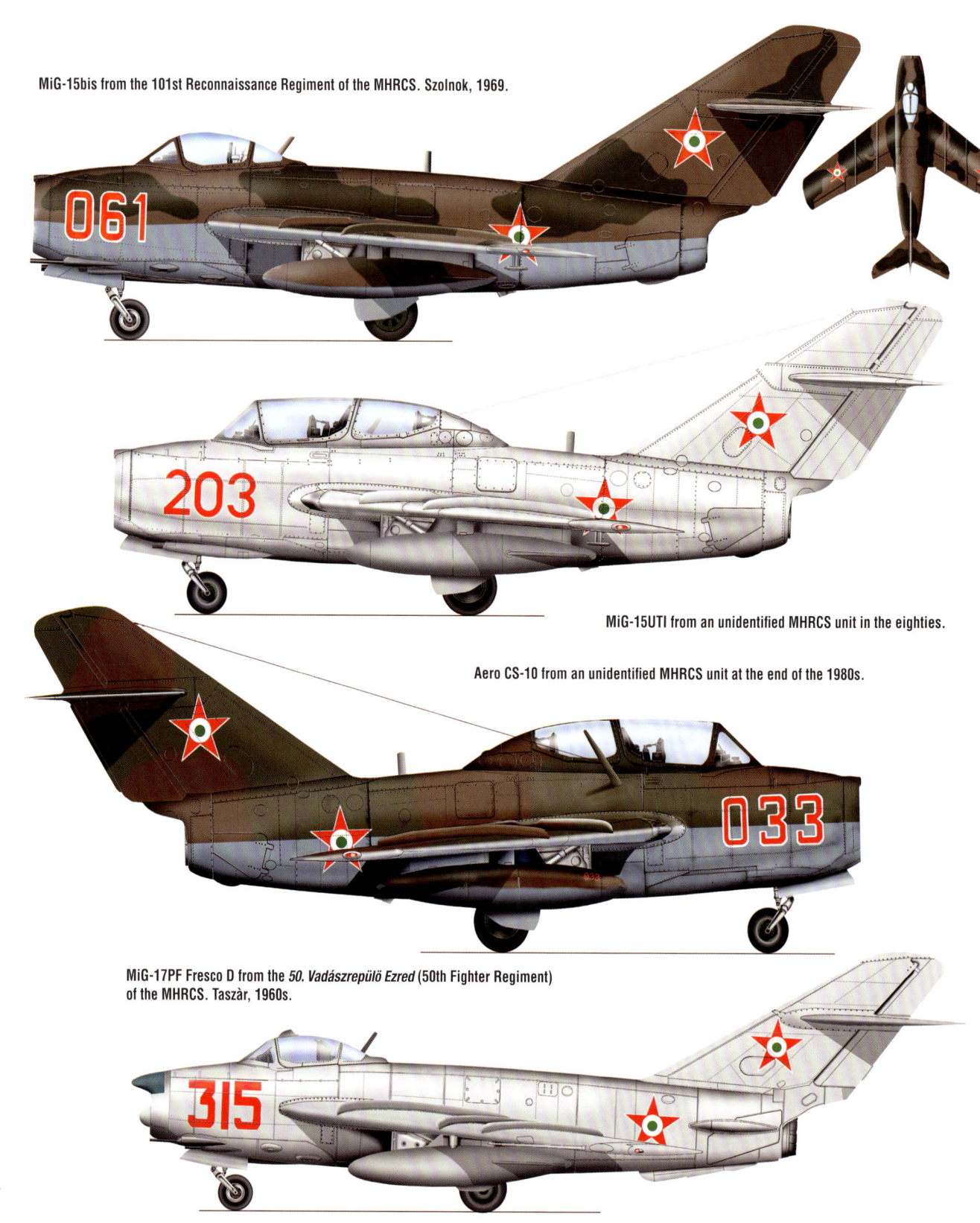

MiG-15bis from the 101st Reconnaissance Regiment of the MHRCS. Szolnok, 1969.

MiG-15UTI from an unidentified MHRCS unit in the eighties.

Aero CS-10 from an unidentified MHRCS unit at the end of the 1980s.

MiG-17PF Fresco D from the *50. Vadászrepülö Ezred* (50th Fighter Regiment) of the MHRCS. Taszàr, 1960s.

MiG-17F 'Fresco C' from the *50. Vadászrepülö Ezred* of the MHRC. Taszàr, 1960s.

# INDONESIA

In 1956 the *Tentara Nasional Indonesia/Angkatan Udara* (TNI/AU – Indonesian Air Force) entered the jet age. This evolution started when the first post-independence president of the republic, Sukarno, was confronted with internal problems and the risk of war with the Malaysian Federation over Dutch New Guinea; in 1958, he launched an air force re-equipment programme.

The rise of the Communist party in Indonesia brought the country closer to the Soviet bloc and it was in this context that a contract was signed at the beginning of 1958 for Jakarta to receive thirty Czech-built C-102 two-seaters for training pilots already flying on MiG-17Fs and MiG-19Ss. This initial delivery was followed in 1958-59 by an extra batch of thirty LIM-5s and seven LIM-5Ps and a large stock of Soviet weaponry was ordered in 1961.

In September 1965, there was a bloody coup d'etat in the capital, Jakarta, and General Soharto put down the Communists pitilessly, forcing President Sokarno to hand over power six months later. Soviet aid to Indonesia dried up and the MiG fleet was quickly grounded because of the lack of spare parts before being withdrawn from service entirely in the middle of the 1970s.

After 1973, Indonesia used only Western machines, in particular F-86 Sabres and T-33s.

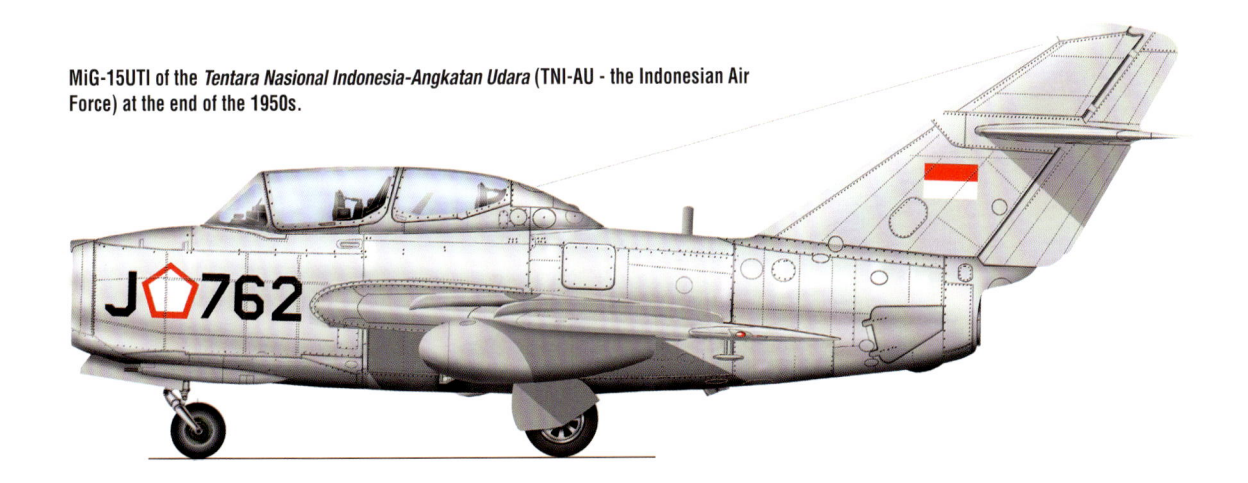

MiG-15UTI of the *Tentara Nasional Indonesia-Angkatan Udara* (TNI-AU - the Indonesian Air Force) at the end of the 1950s.

45

Lim-5 from the 'Thunders', the TNI-AU Aerobatic Team attached to the *Skadron Udara 11* (11th Fighter Squadron) 1960.

Lim-5P from the 'Thunders', *Skadron Udara 11* in 1960.

# IRAQ

After the *coup d'etat* in July 1958 which overthrew the monarchy and brought General Kassem and his Communist partners to power, the new Iraqi government got closer to the Warsaw Pact Countries which meant that there was a halt to arms imports from the West, in particular Great Britain. As a result the *Al Quwwat al-Jawwiya al-Iraqiya*, the Iraqi Air Force, received twenty-odd Soviet- and Czech-built MiG-15bis and thirty or so MiG-15UTIs followed at the beginning of the sixties by a hundred-odd MiG-17Fs and about twenty MiG-17PFs.

Following a further *coup d'etat* in 1963 which overthrew General Kassem, Iraq became closer to NATO and received several modernised British Hawker Hunters which meant that the MiG-17s could be withdrawn from its air force. Other contracts were signed with Great Britain in 1964 but the USSR nonetheless remained the main source of supplies for Iraq, which received more modern MiG variants (MiG-19 and MiG-21, etc.) from 1966 onwards.

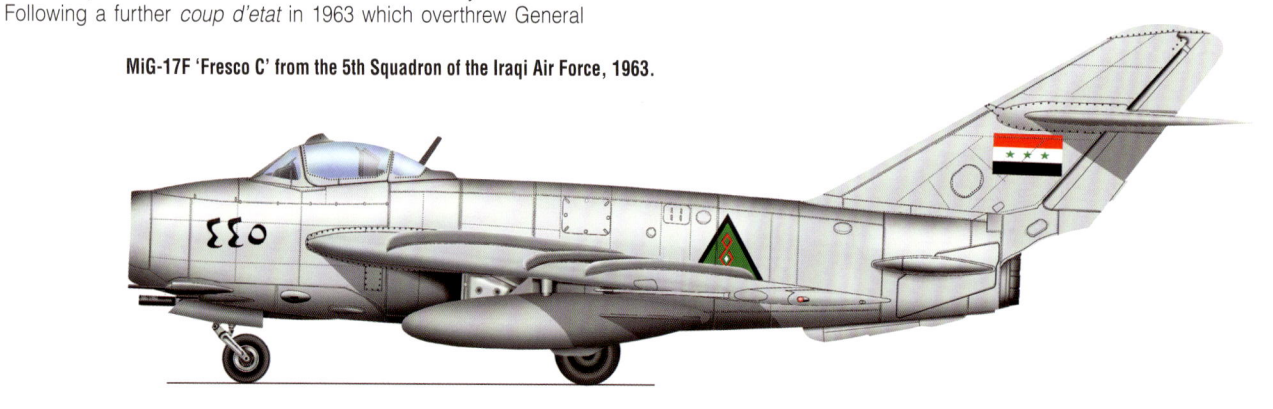

MiG-17F 'Fresco C' from the 5th Squadron of the Iraqi Air Force, 1963.

MiG-15UTI of the *Al Quwwat al-Jawwiya al-Iraqiya*, the Iraqi Air Force, in the 1960s.

MiG-15UTI from an unidentified Iraqi Air Force unit in the 1970s.

MiG-17PF 'Fresco D' of the 7th Squadron of the Iraqi Air Force, 1967.

47

# NORTH KOREA

In June 1950 the first ever fighting between jet planes took place during the war between the People's Democratic Republic of Korea (North Korea), supported by the Soviet Union and China, and the Republic of Korea (South Korea) supported by the United Nations, especially the United States.

MiG-15s flown by Soviet and Polish pilots indeed took on the American F-86 Sabres, in particular in a region which leant itself to aerial combat, near the River Yalu on the border between China and North Korea, quickly called 'MiG Alley'. The Soviet pilots were based on Chinese airfields in Manchuria, and an anti-aircraft defence network was set up along the Yalu to dissuade the Allied Forces from attacking the Chinese aerodromes.

When the war ceased in July 1953, the Korean People's Army's Air Force consisted of several hundred MiG-15bis and MiG-15UTIs which were left behind on the spot by the Soviet units which had used them during the war. The MiG-15bis remained the main front-line fighter in North Korea until it was replaced by the MiG-17 and MiG-19. As for the Midget, about thirty examples may still be in service in the country.

In 1956 the first Soviet-built MiG-17F Fresco Cs appeared in North Korea, as well as some Shenyang F-5s (the export version of the Shenyang J-5), followed in 1958 by MiG-17F Fresco Ds. Deliveries continued and nowadays 200 Shenyang F-5s and FT-5s (the two-seat trainer) are apparently still in service in the Korean People's Army Air Force.

**Korean People's Army Air Force MiG-15 UTI in the 1970s.**

**MiG-15bis of the 177. IAP (177th Soviet Fighter Regiment), Antung, 1951. The pilot of this 'Fagot B', Captain Nikolay Vorobyov was the first Soviet pilot to shoot down an F-86A Sabre (from the 4th Fighter Wing) on 22 December 1950.**

MiG-15 from the 324. IAD (324th Fighter Division). Antung, April 1951.

MiG-15bis of the 523. IAD. Tatung-Kao, October 1951. This fighter's pilot Lieutenant A. Samylov obtained ten kills during the Korean War by shooting down one B-29, two F-84s and seven F-86 Sabres!

MiG-15bis of the 913. IAD in June 1953.

49

MiG-15bis of the 913. IAD. Antung, May 1953. Pilot: Major A. Fedorets (seven kills during the Korean War, all F-86 Sabres).

MiG-15bis

Mig-15 bis. Corée du Nord, 1953.

MiG-17F 'Fresco C', North Korea, 1970s.

MiG-17PF 'Fresco D', North Korea, 1970s.

# MALI

In the middle of the sixties, Mali received military aid from the USSR which in 1965 took the form of a MiG-15UTI trainer and five MiG-17F Fresco Cs for the *Force Aérienne de la République du Mali*. The machines came from Soviet or Czech stocks and were assigned to a squadron based at Bamako-Sénou. Several others were replaced between 1971 and 1974 before the arrival of MiG-21s in 1985-86. During the so-called 'Agacher Strip War', also called the 'Christmas War', the *Force Aérienne de la République du Mali* used its MIG-17Fs in attacks against a certain number of enemy targets.

At the beginning of the nineties, the little fleet of Mali's MiG-17Fs was left to its fate on the bases at Bamako-Sénou and Mopti-Sévaré, but one MiG-17F was put on display at the entry of the Bamako-Sénou Air Force Base.

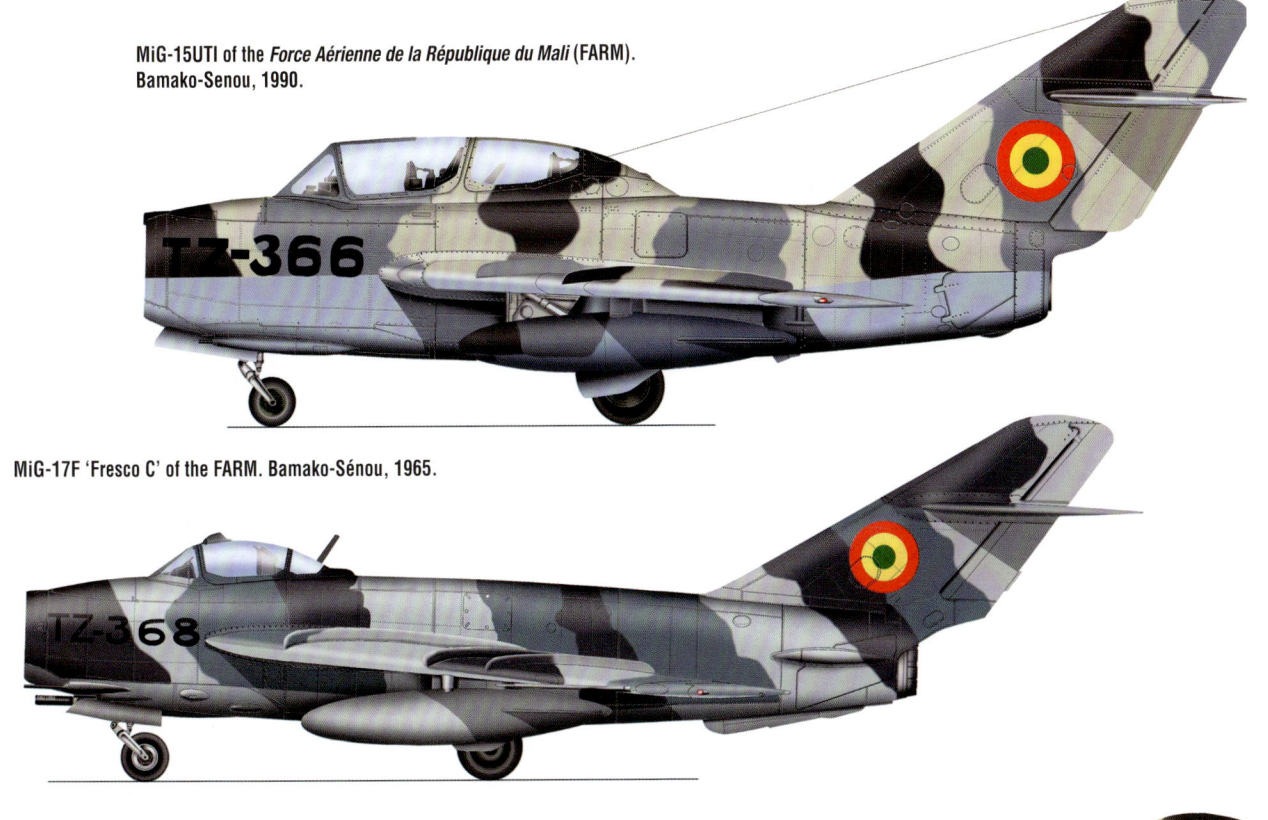

**MiG-15UTI of the *Force Aérienne de la République du Mali* (FARM). Bamako-Senou, 1990.**

**MiG-17F 'Fresco C' of the FARM. Bamako-Sénou, 1965.**

**FARM MiG-17F. N°102 Air Base, Mopti-Sévaré, 1965. This 'Fresco F' bears no roundels either on or underneath the wings.**

# MONGOLIA (People's Republic of)

In 1970 several MiG-15bis and MiG-UTIs as well as some MiG-17 Frescoes appeared in the Mongolian People's Army Air Force. After the arrival of the MiG-21 at the beginning of the eighties, the MiG-15UTIs remained in service until 1986 in an air force which had more than 150 planes of different types of which ten or so were MiG-17F Fresco Cs which were used until the beginning of the nineties.

**Mongolian People's Army Air Force MiG-17 Fresco A.**

# MOZAMBIQUE

Set up when Mozambique gained its independence in 1975, the *Forca Aérea de Moçambique*, or FAM, was renamed *Força Popular Aérea de Moçambique* between 1985 and 1990.

Backed by the USSR and Cuba, Mozambique received a certain number of MiG-15UTIs and thirty-odd MiG-17 Fresco As, MiG-17F Fresco Cs and Polish LIM-5s at the beginning of the eighties to help the government during the civil war that ravaged the country from 1977 to 1992. These planes remained in service at least until 1991.

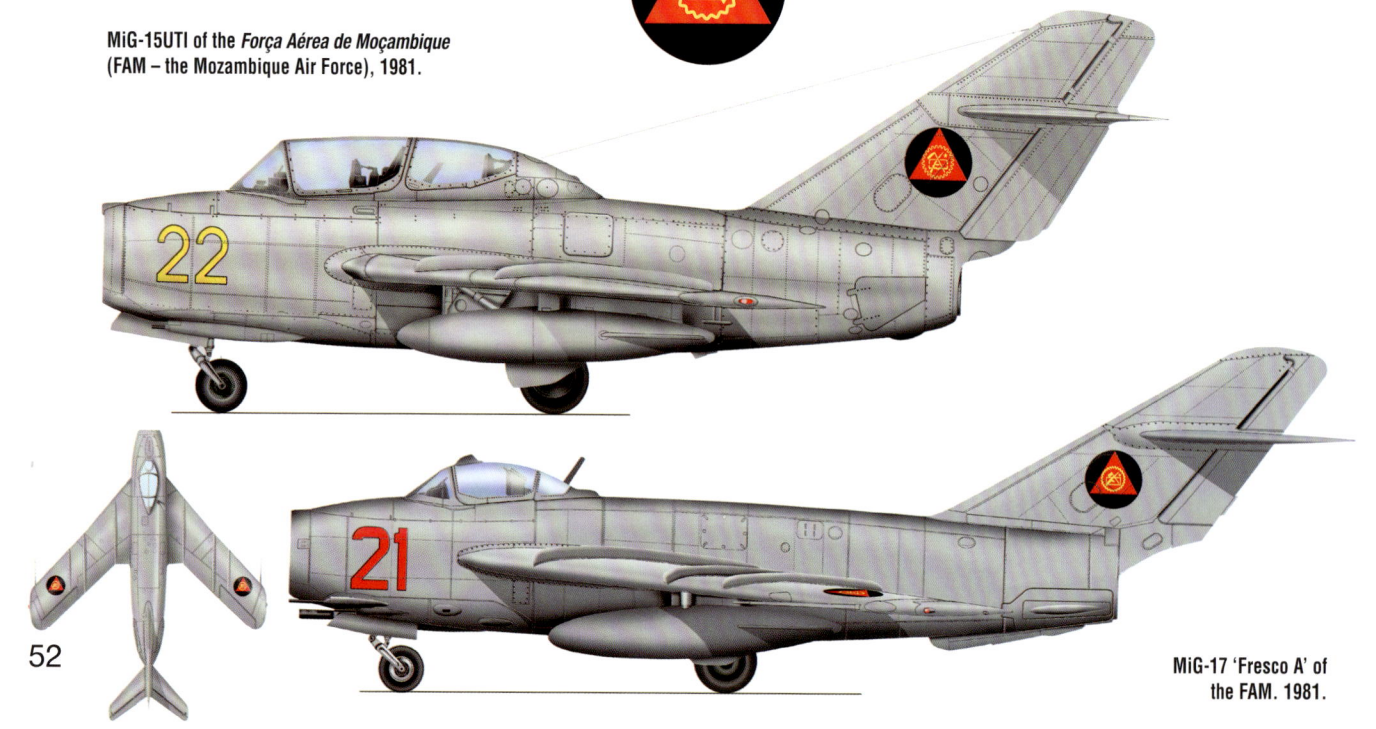

**MiG-15UTI of the *Força Aérea de Moçambique* (FAM – the Mozambique Air Force), 1981.**

**MiG-17 'Fresco A' of the FAM. 1981.**

# NIGERIA

In 1967 during the Biafran War – or the Nigerian Civil War which broke out in July 1967 and ended in 1970 by Biafra being reinstated into Nigeria – the Soviet Union delivered ten or so MiG-17 F Fresco As and a few MiG-15UTIs to the Nigerian Air Force (NAF) which then used the bases at Kano airport in the northern part of the country.

Subsequently thirty or so MiG-17s joined the NAF whose Fresco As came from the LSK/LV (East Germany's air force), together with some former Egyptian MiG-17F Fresco Cs. The latter remained in service until 1975 when they were replaced by MiG-21s. The MiG-15UTIs were still operational in the middle of the eighties.

MiG-15UTI of the Nigerian Air Force (NAF), Kano, 1967.

MiG-17F 'Fresco C', delivered to the NAF in April 1968.

NAF MiG-17F 'Fresco C', based at Enugu during the Biafran War, 1969.

# PAKISTAN

After setting up close ties with China in 1950, Pakistan received constant help from this country for military equipment. It was in this context that the *Pakistan Fiza'ya* (Pakistan Air Force) received several Shenyang F-2s and MiG-15bis from Chinese stocks, as well as some Shenyang FT-2 trainers (MiG-15UTIs) which were based at Mianwali in the northwest of the Punjab.

Pakistan used one version of the MiG-17 only, the Shenyang-FT-5, delivered in 1975 and assigned to the 1st Fighter Conversion Unit (FCU), also based at Mianwali. These machines were withdrawn from service in 2012 but had been replaced since 1995 by some Nanghang/ PAC K-8 Karakorums produced by Pakistan and China in partnership.

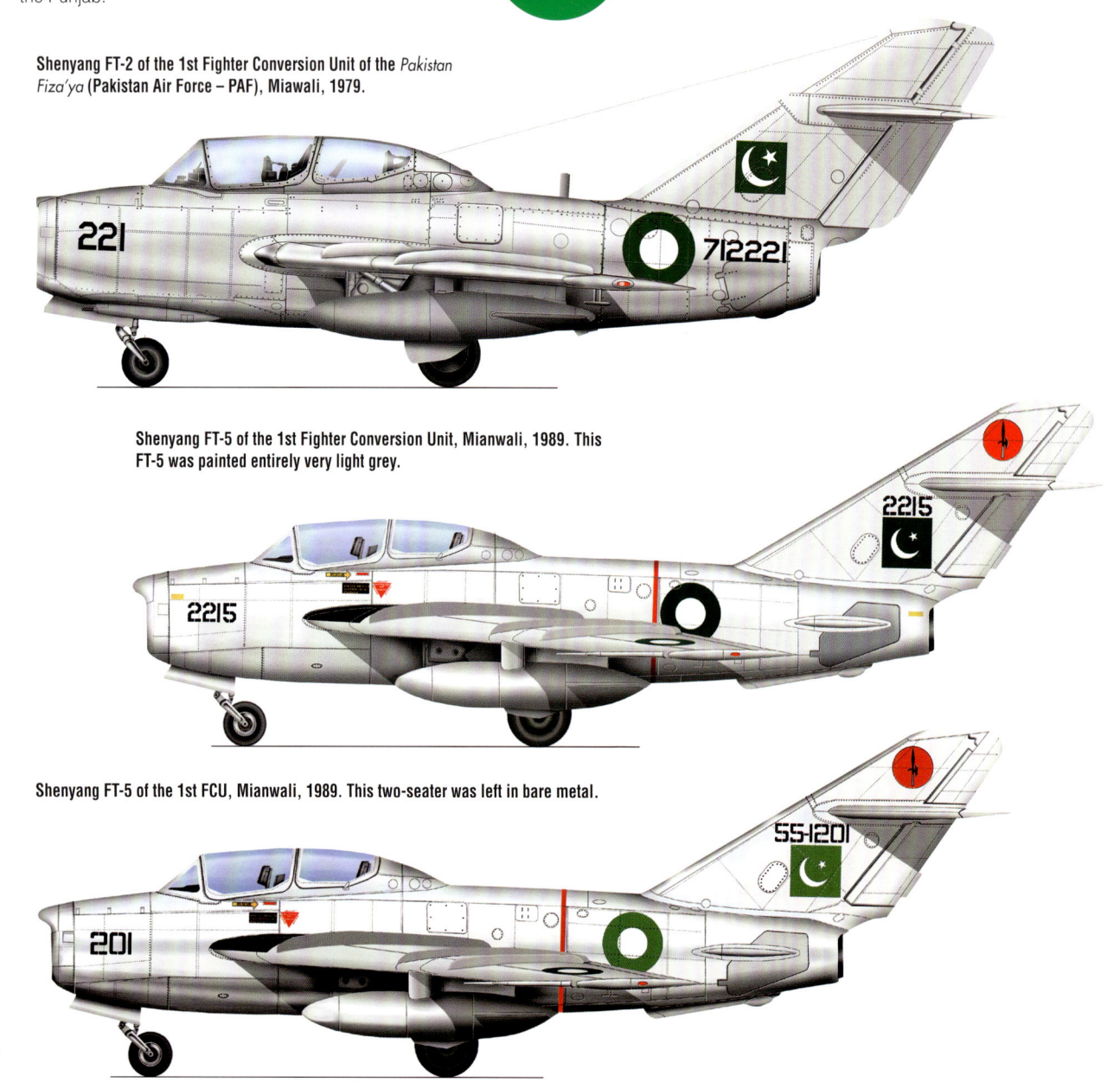

**Shenyang FT-2 of the 1st Fighter Conversion Unit of the** *Pakistan Fiza'ya* **(Pakistan Air Force – PAF), Miawali, 1979.**

**Shenyang FT-5 of the 1st Fighter Conversion Unit, Mianwali, 1989. This FT-5 was painted entirely very light grey.**

**Shenyang FT-5 of the 1st FCU, Mianwali, 1989. This two-seater was left in bare metal.**

Shenyang FT-5 of the 1st FCU. Mianwali, 1990.

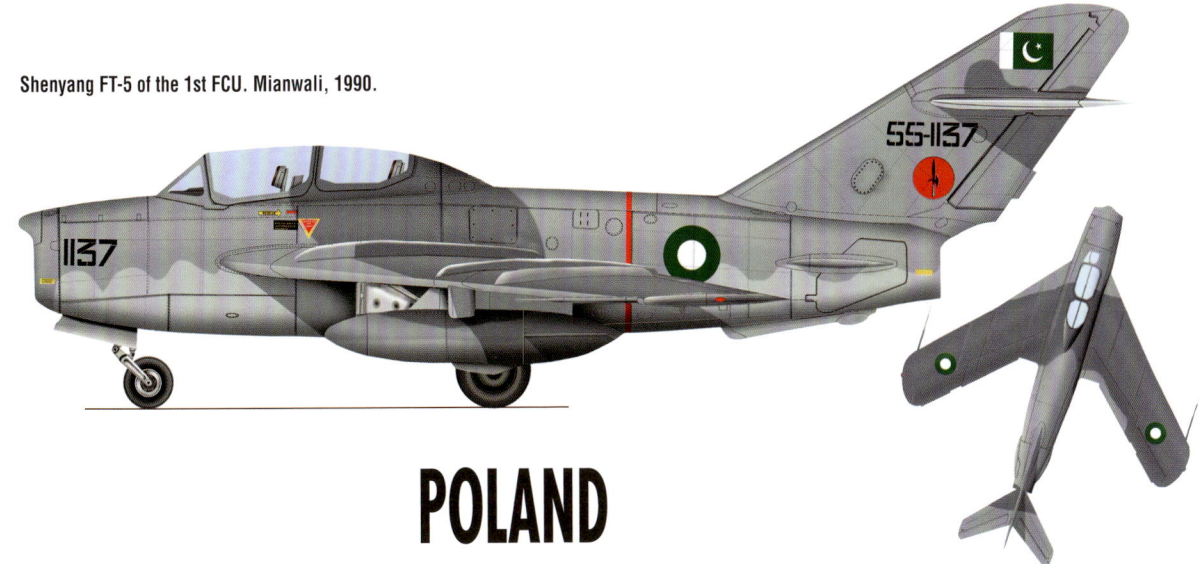

# POLAND

## MiG-15

The *Polskie Wojsko Lotnicze* (PWL - Polish Air Force) started to put the MiG-15 into service in June 1951 when the first examples of the type were delivered by the Soviet Union to the 1st Fighter Regiment (*1. Pulk Lotnictwa Mysliwskiego*) 'Warsawa', based near Minsk-Mazowiecki and given the task of protecting the country's capital, Warsaw. A short while earlier, licence-built production at the PZL (*Panstwowe Zaklady Lotnicze*) factory at Mielec had been given the green light by the Soviet Union. The first aircraft assembled from USSR-supplied parts were called Lim-1 (literally 'licence-built fighter' N°1) and they went into service in the PWL fighter units at the end of 1952.

At the same time, thirty-odd MiG-15bis were delivered by the USSR to Polish fighter units; this version was then itself built under licence locally under the name Lim-2, these new fighters entering service at the end of 1954.

The Polish Air Force which had received some MiG-15UTI trainers and some Czech-built Aero CS-102s was then equipped with SB Lim-1s and SB Lim-2s – Lim-1s converted into two-seat trainers. In 1970, the Lim-2 was still in service in Poland, mainly as a fighter-bomber whereas the MiG-15UTIs continued their career until into the eighties.

## MiG-17

Poland put its first MiG-17PF Fresco Ds delivered by the USSR into service in 1955, these interceptors being used until the middle of the sixties. When the Lim-5 (MiG-17F Fresco C) was built under licence in the country, it became the most used aircraft in the PWL. As for the Lim-5P (Mig-17PF Fresco D built under licence) all-weather fighter, it entered service in 1959 and was only withdrawn from service twenty years later. Poland also put some Lim-5M tactical fighters into front line service in 1960, these planes being transformed into standard Lim-6bis four years later. Moreover, a photographic reconnaissance version was also produced locally under the name of Lim-5MR. Still for the reconnaissance role, forty-odd Lim-5s were converted into Lim-5Rs which entered service in July 1960.

Forty examples of the Lim-6, an improved version of the Lim-5M, were built but because of the plane's flight characteristics (including handling when landing and taking off) which were too demanding for fighter pilots, these machines were not put into service in operational front line units. A number of them however were subsequently converted into Lim-6bis.

In 1962, a new fighter-bomber, a modified variant of the Lim-5 was developed under the name of Lim-6. This plane, of which the last

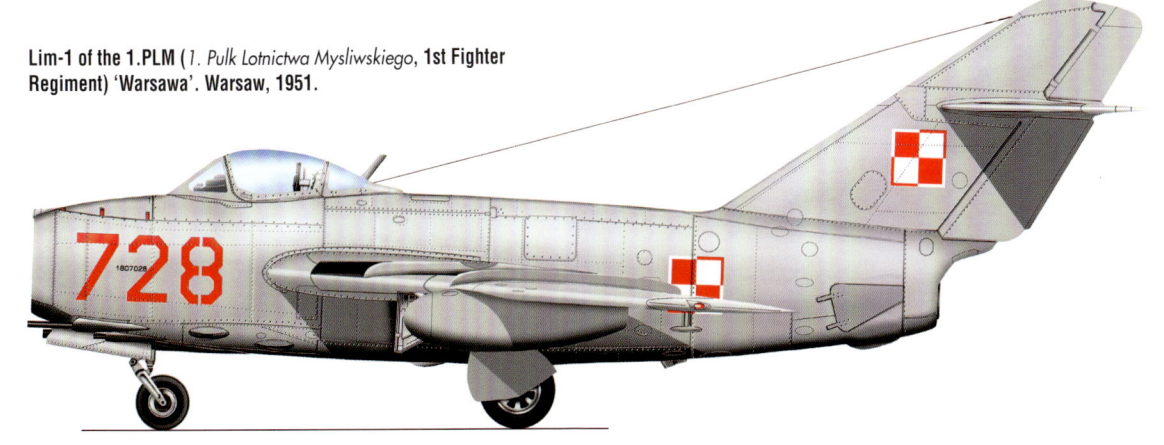

Lim-1 of the 1.PLM (*1. Pulk Lotnictwa Mysliwskiego*, **1st Fighter Regiment**) 'Warsawa'. Warsaw, 1951.

55

**Lim-2 of the 1. PLM. Warsaw, 1954.**

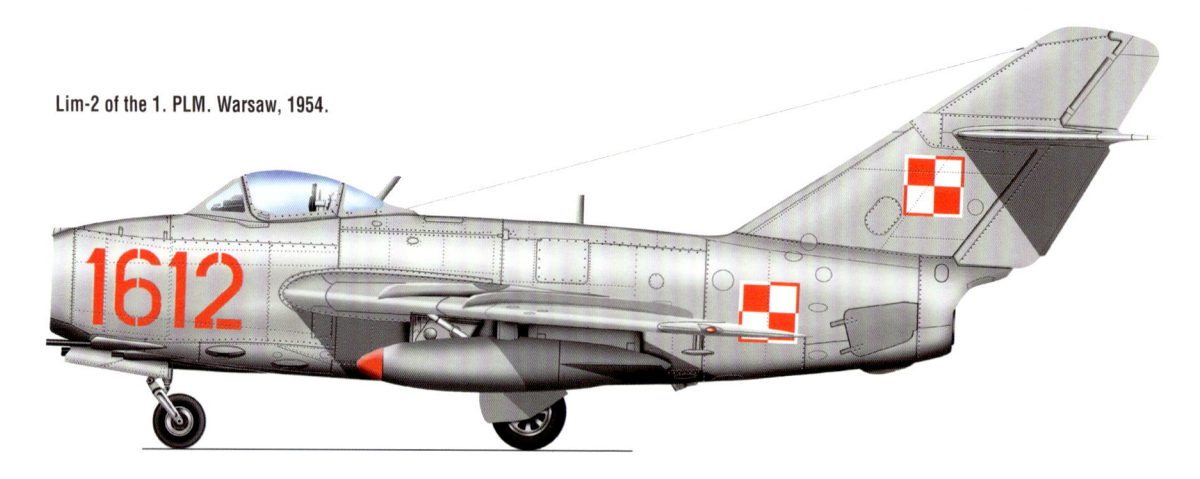

example came off the production lines in February 1964, remained operational in Poland until 1992.

Another reconnaissance version, based on the Lim-6bis, was also produced in 1964 and called the Lim-6R (and Lim-6bisMR).

In 1970, the MiG-21 started replacing the Lim-5 which was therefore transferred to the training units. The last flight by a Lim-5 in Poland took place in July 1993, ending the Fresco's almost forty years of PWL service.

At the beginning of the seventies, forty-odd Lim-5Ps were converted into a ground attack version, the Lim-6M. About fifteen examples of another reconnaissance and attack variant, the Lim-6MR, were also produced and withdrawn from service in 1988.

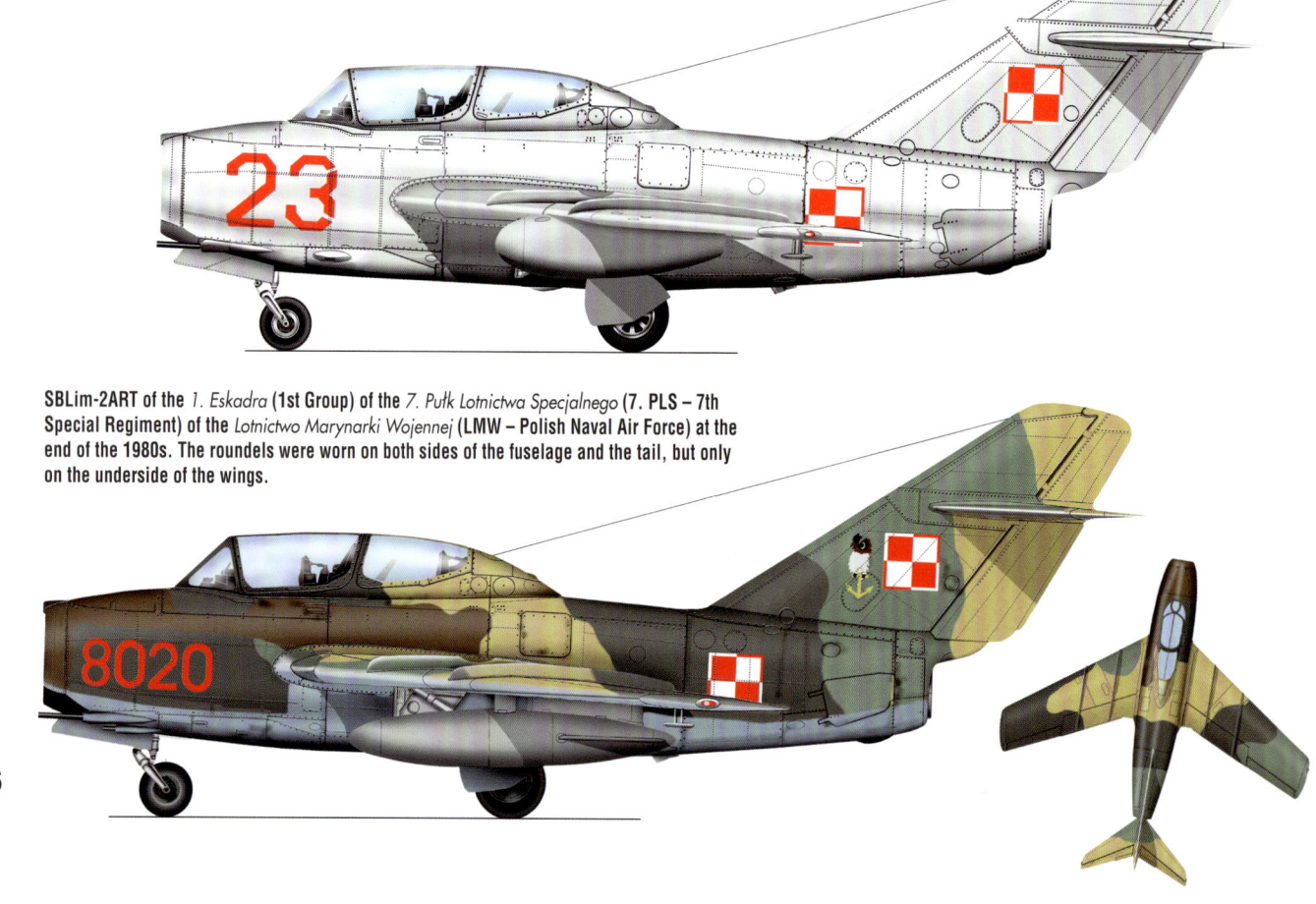

**SBLim-1 from an unidentified** *Polskie Wojsko Lotnicze* **(PWL – Polish Air Force) unit in the 1970s.**

**SBLim-2ART of the** *1. Eskadra* **(1st Group) of the** *7. Pułk Lotnictwa Specjalnego* **(7. PLS – 7th Special Regiment) of the** *Lotnictwo Marynarki Wojennej* **(LMW – Polish Naval Air Force) at the end of the 1980s. The roundels were worn on both sides of the fuselage and the tail, but only on the underside of the wings.**

56

SBLim-2M of the 1. Esk, 7. PLS at the end of the 1980s.

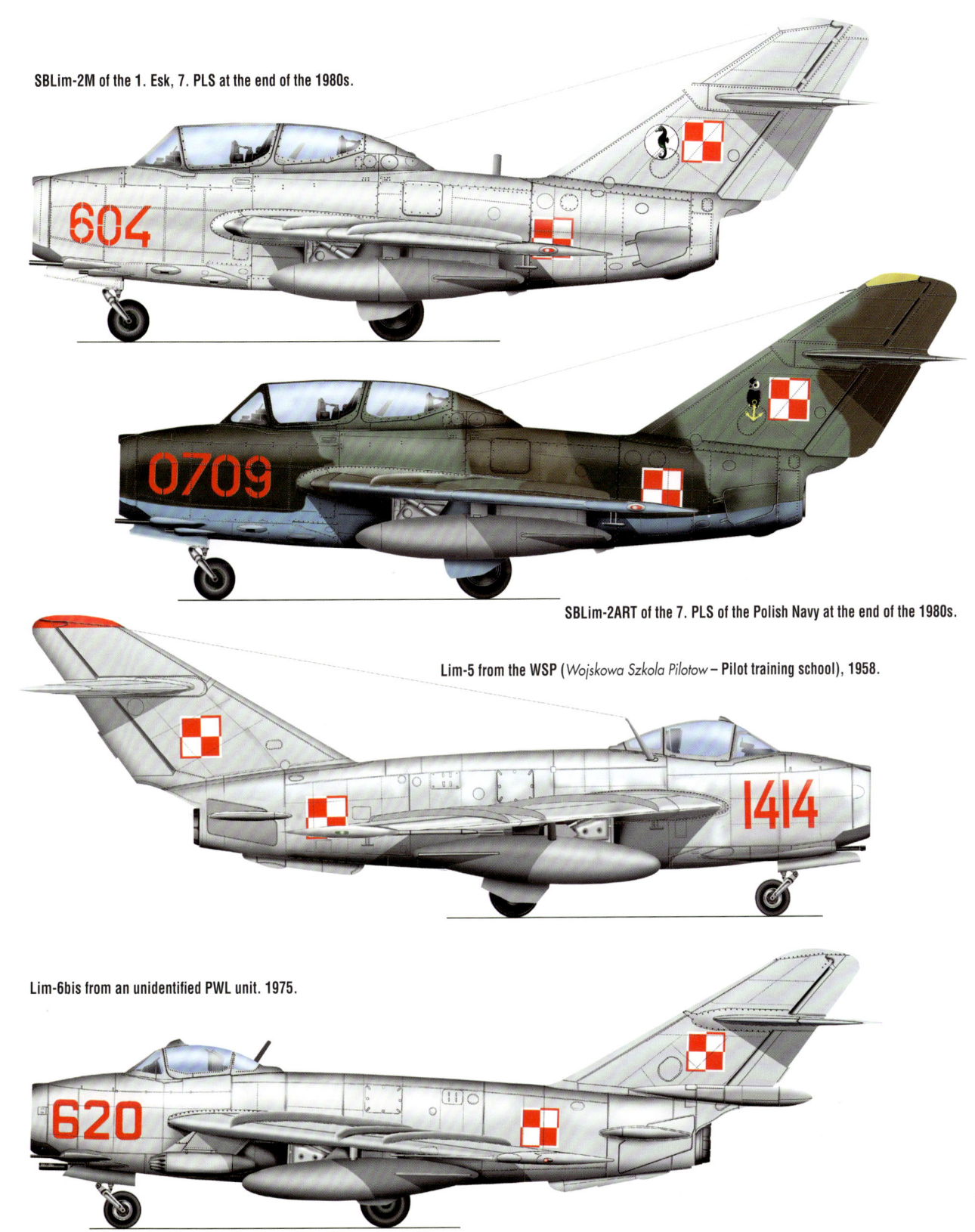

SBLim-2ART of the 7. PLS of the Polish Navy at the end of the 1980s.

Lim-5 from the WSP (*Wojskowa Szkola Pilotow* – Pilot training school), 1958.

Lim-6bis from an unidentified PWL unit. 1975.

57

Lim-6bis (MiG-17F) of the 45. **LPSzB** (*Lotniczy Pułk Szkolno-Bojowy* – **Air Combat Training Regiment**), 1990.

Lim-6bis of the 45. LPSzB. Babimost, 1990.

Lim-6bis of the 45. LPSz-B. Babimost, 1985.

Lim-6bis from the 7. PLS of the Polish Navy. These planes were used as 'aggressors' which explains this unusual camouflage, 1980s.

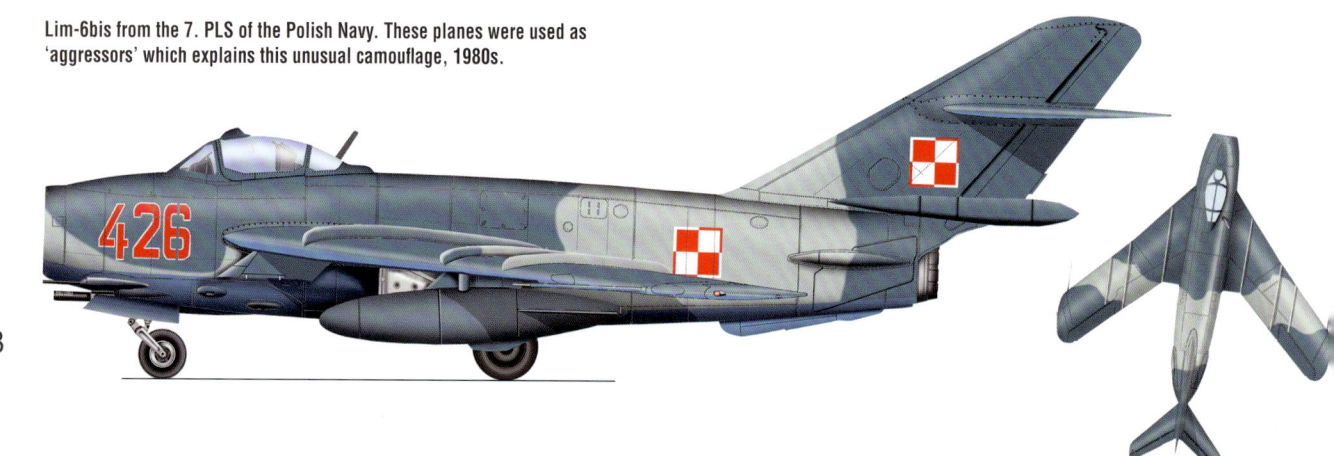

58

**Lim-5P (MiG-17PF) from an unidentified PWL unit at the end of the 1960s.**

**Lim-6M (MiG-17PF) from an unidentified PWL unit, 1971.**

# ROMANIA

## MiG-15

The MiG-15 appeared in the *Fortele Aeriene ale Republicii Socialiste Române* (Romanian Air Force) at the beginning of the fifties, with almost 160 examples of this fighter being delivered to this country together with more than 200 Czech-built Aero S-102s. In the middle of the 1950s, fifty or so MiG-15bis were used as fighter-bombers, with Romania also using a hundred or so MiG-15UTI and Aero CS-102 two-seat trainers.

A dozen or so MiG-15bis and MiG-15UTIs were still in service for tactical training at the beginning of the nineties before being finally withdrawn from service. After withdrawal, some S-102s, S-103s and CS-102s were kept and put on display in various museums.

## MiG-17

In 1955, a dozen MiG-17PF Fresco Ds were delivered to Romania, joined a year later by the same number of MiG-17F Fresco Cs. These fighters were used alongside the MiG-15s in mixed fighter regiments during the fifties and sixties but at the beginning of the 1990s, the ten or so surviving MiG-17s were used as tactical trainers.

When withdrawn from service, several Frescoes likewise made their way into various Romanian museums.

**Aero S-102 from an unidentified unit of the** *Fortele Aeriene ale Republicii Socialiste Române* **(Romanian Socialist Republic Air Force – FARSR), Devselu, 1962.**

59

MiG-15bis from an unidentified FARSR unit in the 1960s.

MiG-15bis from an unidentified FARSR unit in 1995.

Aero CS-102 from an unidentified FARSR unit in 1954.

Aero CS-102 from an unidentified unit of the *Fortele Aeriene ale Romaniei* (**FAR** – Romanian Air Force, the new name adopted in 1989). This type of roundel worn from 1915 to 1941 and then from 1944 to 1950 was reintroduced in 1984. This two-seater was painted light grey-blue all over.

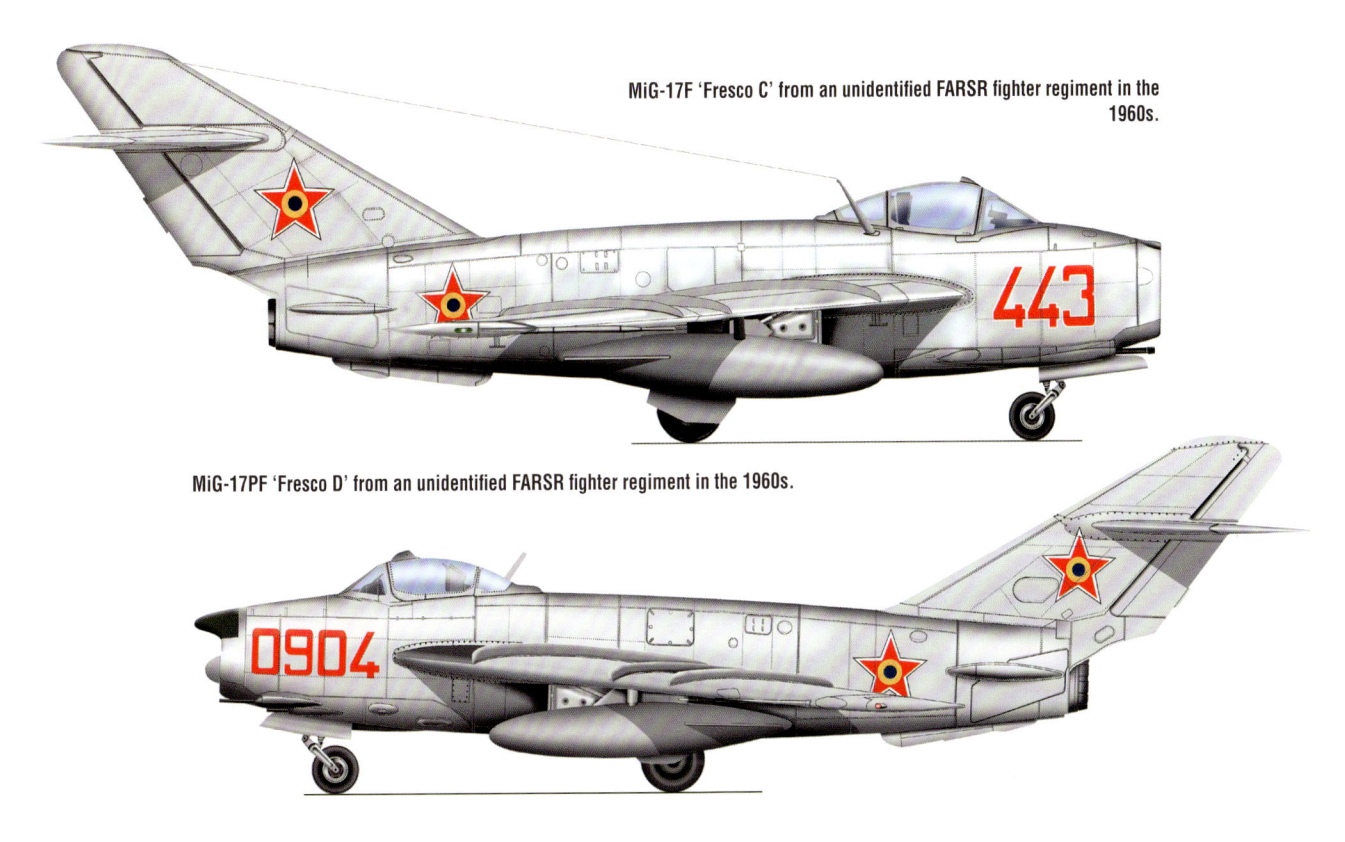

MiG-17F 'Fresco C' from an unidentified FARSR fighter regiment in the 1960s.

MiG-17PF 'Fresco D' from an unidentified FARSR fighter regiment in the 1960s.

# SOMALIA

Because of its close ties with the Soviet bloc, Somalia received some MiG-15UTIs and MiG-17 Fresco As in 1963 to equip its air force (the *Ciidanka Cirka Soomaaliyed* or CCS). The Somali MiG-17s and MiG-21s were not used very much before the Ogaden War which began when Somali troops invaded this Ethiopian region in July 1977 to incorporate it into a 'Greater Somalia'.

Soviet aid had stopped in August 1977 because the Somalis had progressed beyond the Ogaden border and the Somali military situation became critical the following November, mainly because of a lack of reinforcements and supplies.

The Somali government decided therefore to dismiss the Soviet advisors still present in the country, which made the USSR change sides and supply Ethiopia with massive aid. The situation was reversed again in February 1978 and the war ended with Ethiopia winning.

After this conflict, Somalia had lost all its air force, mostly through accidents. A small number of MiG-17s however continued to fly thanks to spare parts bought off China who also supplied Somalia with some Shenyang F-6 fighters and FT-6 trainers.

MiG-15UTI of the *Ciidanka Cirka Soomaaliyed* (CCS – Somali Air Force). Mogadisciu, 1992.

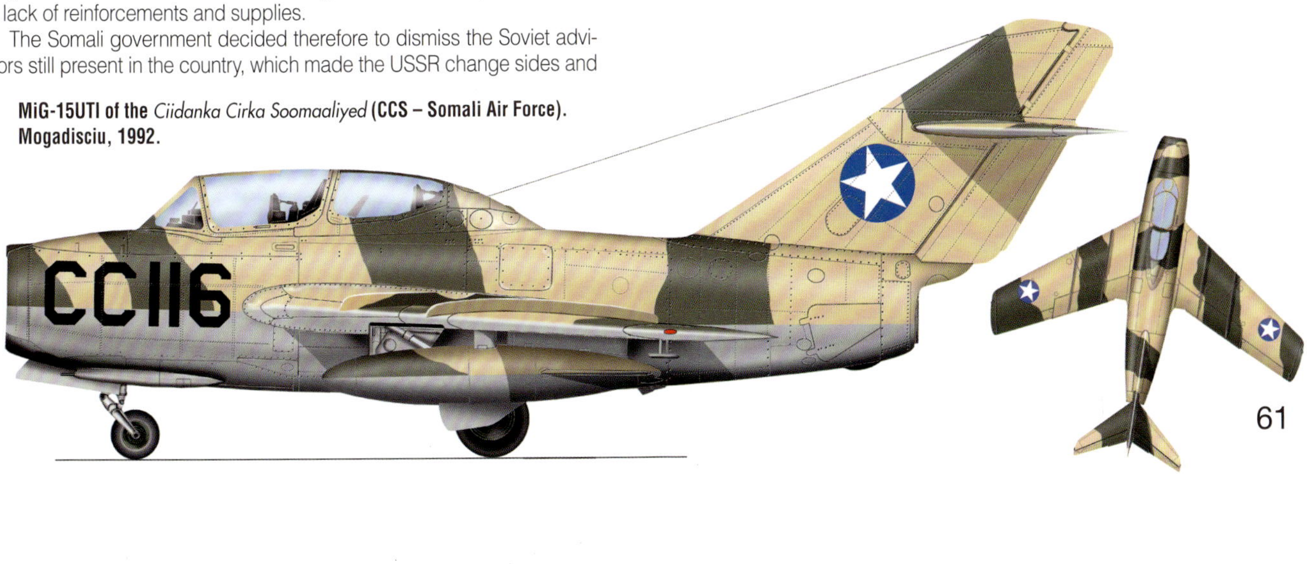

**Somali Air Force MiG-17 'Fresco A' at the end of the 1980s.**

**Somali Air Force MiG-17 during the Ogaden War, 1977.**

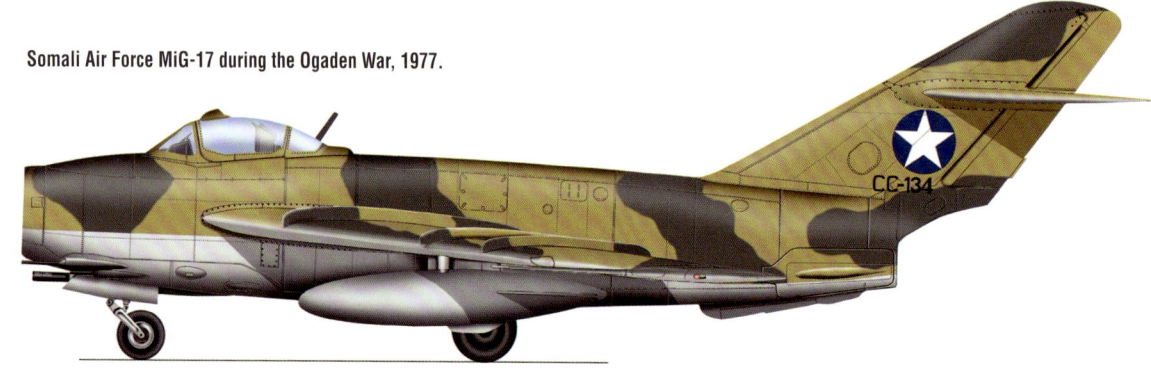

**Somali Air Force MiG-17 during the Ogaden War, 1977.**

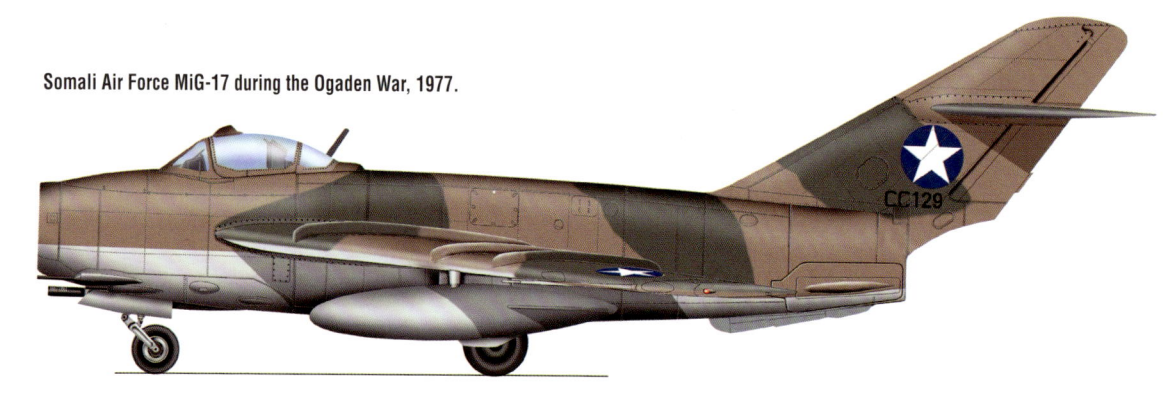

# SOVIET UNION

It was at the beginning of the Cold War in 1947 that the MiG-15 was developed by the USSR to equip its air force (the V-VS). The 324th Air Defence Interception Division based at Kubinka was the first unit to be declared operational on this fighter, at the beginning of 1949. A year after the MiG-15 was put into service, the '*Krasnaya Pyaterka*' (Red Five), an acrobatic team made up of five entirely red machines, was created at Kubinka. At the beginning of the fifties, several MiG-15 units were deployed permanently in Poland, East Germany and Hungary. The MiG-15UTI played an important part in training young pilots from Soviet air force front-line units and those from foreign air forces equipped with the same type of plane. The Midget also helped flying techniques to evolve and pilots to qualify operationally. From 1950 till the middle of the 1970s, the MiG-15s were involved in a lot of incidents involving spy planes entering Soviet air space, shooting down some of them and suffering some losses themselves.

At the time when the V-VS re-equipped with MiG-17s, the MiG-15s were relegated to the fighter-bomber role. The MiG-17 Fresco A entered USSR service in 1952 and very quickly became an important

MiG-15bis from an unidentified unit of the V-VS (Voyenno-vozdushnye sily – Military Air Forces) of the URSS at the beginning of the 1950s.

element in the Soviet Air Force. The MiG-15UTI was used for conversion and perfecting Fresco pilots for whom a two-seat version was never made in the Soviet Union.

During the following years, the MiG-17s and the MiG-17F Fresco C were mainly used as tactical fighters and for air defence, and in 1955 the tactical division of the V-VS and that of the Air Defence of the PVO (*Protivo-Vozdushnaya Oborona* - air defence force) numbered some 2000 MiG-17s of all sorts in their units. Their role was to defend the borders of the country against Western reconnaissance aircraft whose incursions were very frequent.

After the Soviet Air Force was reorganised in the middle of the fifties, the ground attack division was disbanded and replaced in 1957 by a fighter-bomber division. With the arrival of new fighters, the MiG-17 became obsolete and several Fresco units were transferred to the fighter-bomber division, the planes being then armed with rockets and bombs.

The 'Reds Five' acrobatic team was re-equipped with five new MiG-17s replacing the MiG-15bis it had flown until then.

In 1954, the Soviet fighter regiments equipped with MiG-17s and not MiG-15s were based in Poland and East Germany. Fresco As were also deployed in Czechoslovakia when the country was invaded by Warsaw Pact Countries in August 1968 to put and end to the Prague Uprising.

The career of the MiG-17 in the USSR continued well into the 1990s, when the fighter was still in service in several independent fighter units.

MiG-15bis from an unidentified unit of the DOSAAF (the Association for Volunteers to Assist the Army), a Soviet paramilitary organisation which was given most of the MiG-15s and MiG-15bis after they were withdrawn from front-line service. The fuselage star was not worn after 1955.

MiG-15bis from the 'Red Five' aerobatic team, Kubinka, 1955.

MiG-15 from the 'Red Five' aerobatic team. Kubinka, 1950.

MiG-15UTI from an unidentified VVS unit. This 'Midget' bore the identification stripes worn during the Soviet 1968 intervention in Czechoslovakia.

MiG-17 'Fresco A' from an unidentified VVS unit having taken part in the Soviet intervention in Czechoslovakia in August 1968.

64

MiG-17PM 'Fresco E' from an unidentified VVS unit in 1955. This version was armed with four RS-1-U (AA-1 'Alkali') missiles.

MiG-17 'Fresco A' from an unidentified VVS unit in the 1960s. This fighter bears the medium grey camouflage used by Soviet MiG-17s.

MiG-17F 'Fresco C' of the DOSAAF.

MiG-17 'Fresco A' from the 'Red Five' aerobatic team, 1955.

65

MiG-17F 'Fresco C' assigned to the Kiev district, 1970.

MiG-17PF Fresco D from the 146. GvIAP (146th Fighter Regiment of the Guard). Vasilkov, 1957.

# SUDAN

After gaining its independence in 1956, Sudan set up its air force with the help of the British who supplied it with military equipment and assistance. At the end of the sixties, the Sudanese government turned to the Soviet Union and China to equip its air force (the *Al Quwwat al-Jawwiya as-Sudaniyya*) and received several Shenyang JJ-2s, some MiG-15UTIs and twenty or so Shenyang F-5s and FT-5s which were delivered in 1969. A new batch of FT-5s was delivered at the beginning of the eighties, of which some were no longer in flying condition by 2010.

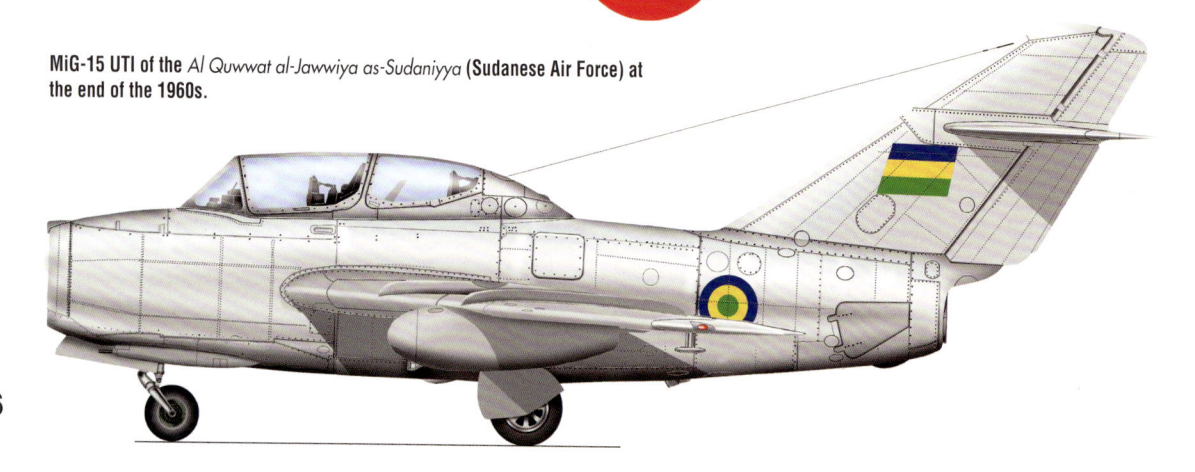

**MiG-15 UTI** of the *Al Quwwat al-Jawwiya as-Sudaniyya* **(Sudanese Air Force)** at the end of the 1960s.

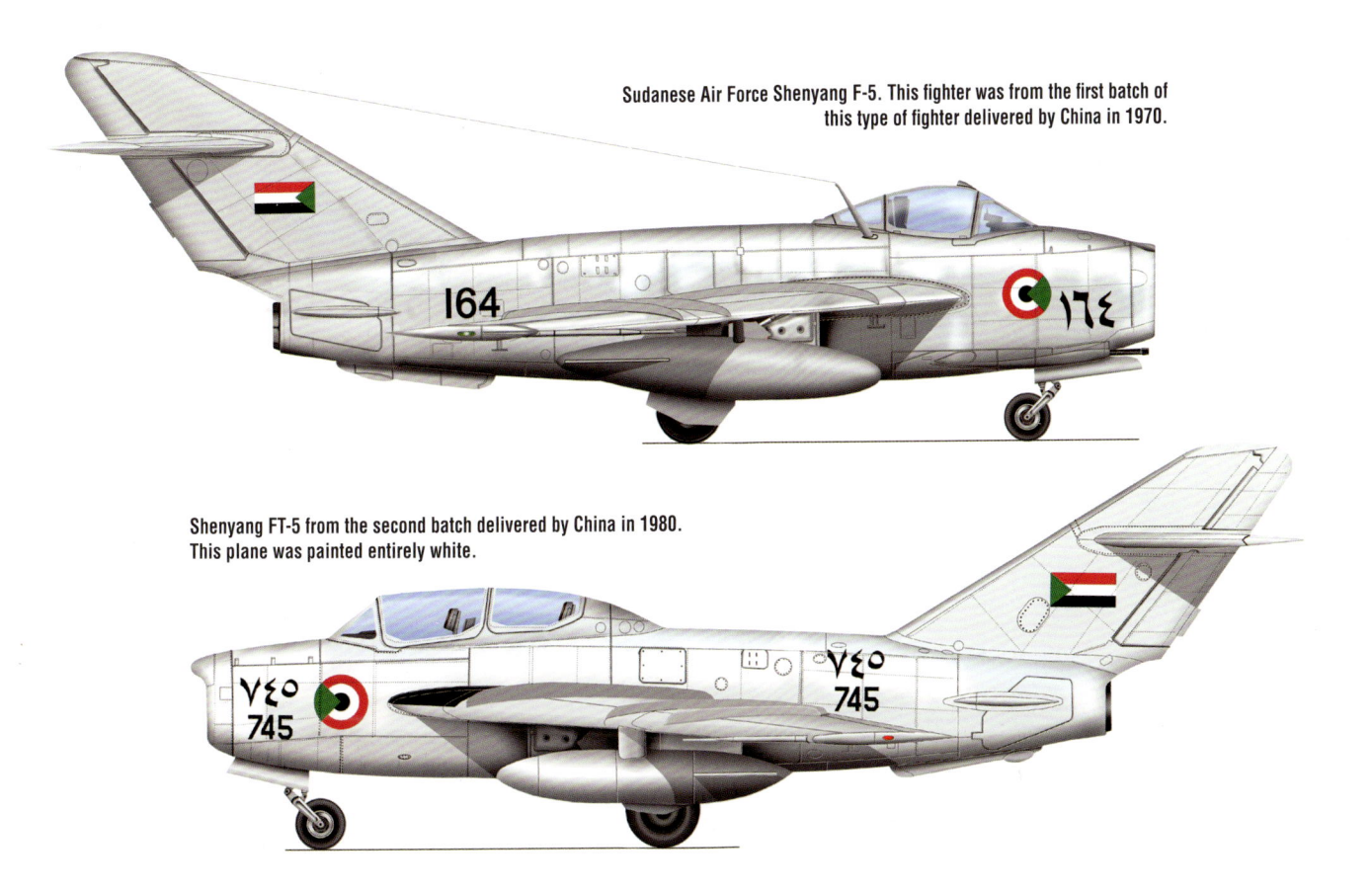

**Sudanese Air Force Shenyang F-5.** This fighter was from the first batch of this type of fighter delivered by China in 1970.

**Shenyang FT-5 from the second batch delivered by China in 1980. This plane was painted entirely white.**

# SRI LANKA

Following an insurrection by the Liberation Tigers of Tamil Ealam (or LTTE) rebels in the spring of 1971, the Sri Lankan government turned to the Soviet Union to obtain more up to date machines than those then in service with its air force, the *Sri Lanka Guwan Hamudawa* – Sri Lanka Air Force, or SLAF. It received one MiG-15UTI and five MiG-17 Fresco As which remained operational in the country until 1979. In 1991, China delivered four Shenyang FT65s to Sri Lanka two of which were subsequently put on display in museums after they were withdrawn from service.

**MiG-15UTI from No 6 Squadron of the *Sri Lanka Guwan Hamudawa* (Sri Lanka Air Force). Colombo-Katunayake, 1979.**

67

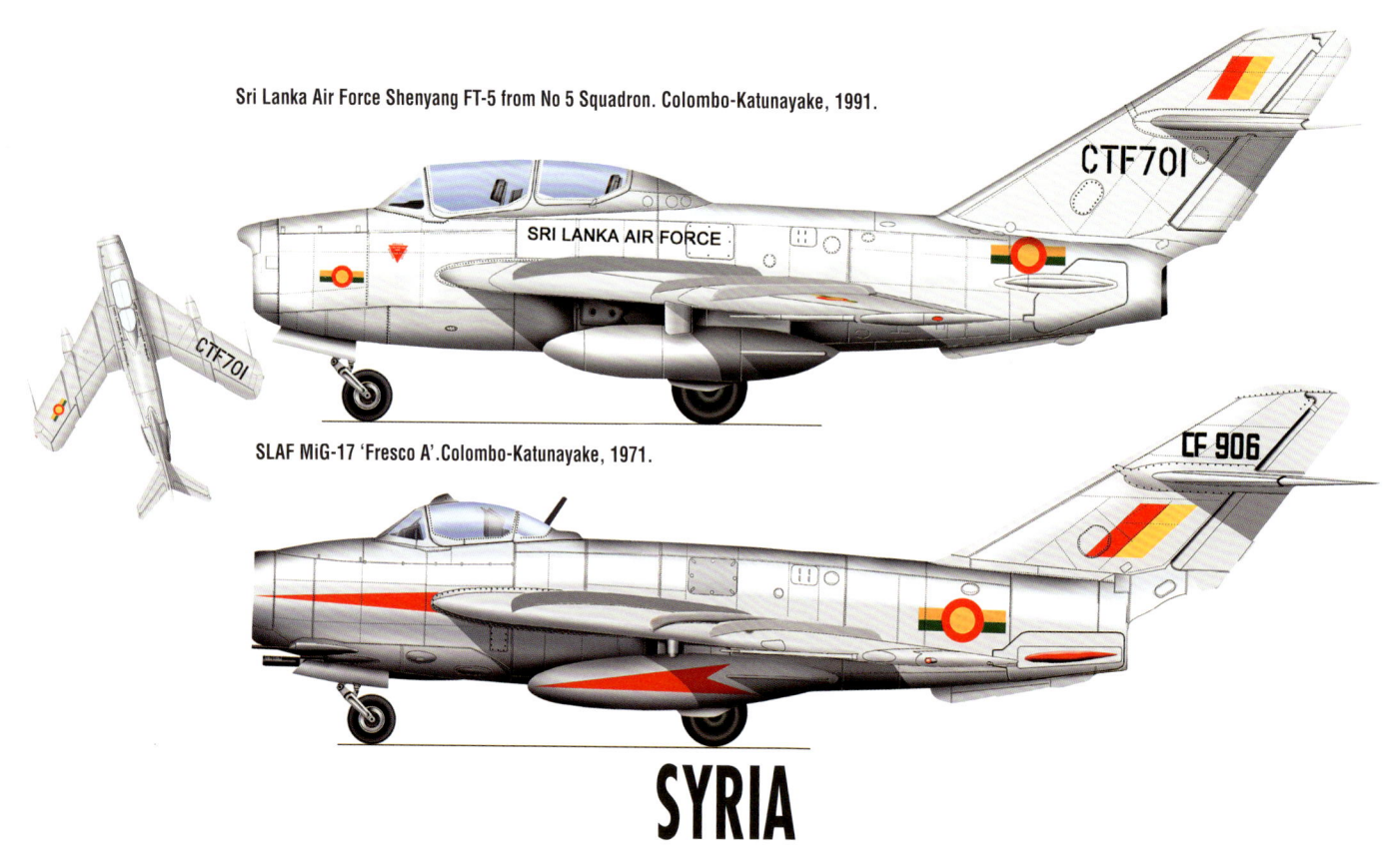

**Sri Lanka Air Force Shenyang FT-5 from No 5 Squadron. Colombo-Katunayake, 1991.**

**SLAF MiG-17 'Fresco A'. Colombo-Katunayake, 1971.**

# SYRIA

In 1955 Syria established relations with Moscow and placed a first order for twenty MiG-15 Fagots and four MiG-15UTIs to equip its air force, the *Al Quwwat al-Jawwiyah al Arabiya as-Souriya*. These machines were delivered by Czechoslovakia to Egypt where the Syrian pilots and mechanics were being trained. However during the Suez Crisis in November 1956, nearly all the machines were destroyed on the ground by strikes made by the Israeli-Franco-British coalition.

Other deliveries followed so that the Syrian MiG-15s – in all about thirty MiG-15s and six MiG-15UTIs – took part in all the clashes with Israel at the time. Between January and August 1957, sixty or so MiG-17F Fresco Cs were delivered to Syria, the planes becoming part of the United Arab Republic (UAR) Air Force, a union which united Syria and Egypt from 1958 to 1961.

Syria started to receive some MiG-21s at the beginning of the sixties, these new planes thereby relegating the MiG-17Fs to the fighter-bomber role.

During the Six-Day War, from 5 to 10 June 1967, the Syrian Air Force lost two-thirds of its fleet, including some MiG-17Fs. The MiG-17F was used for ground support missions escorted by MiG-21s during the Yom Kippur War from 6 to 25 October 1976, and during this conflict several MiG-17Fs were also lost in aerial combat. In 1991 thirty or so MiG-17Fs were still in service in Syria, used mainly for tactical training.

**MiG-15bis of the *Al Quwwat al-Jawwiyah al Arabiya as-Souriya* (Syrian Air Force) in the 1960s.**

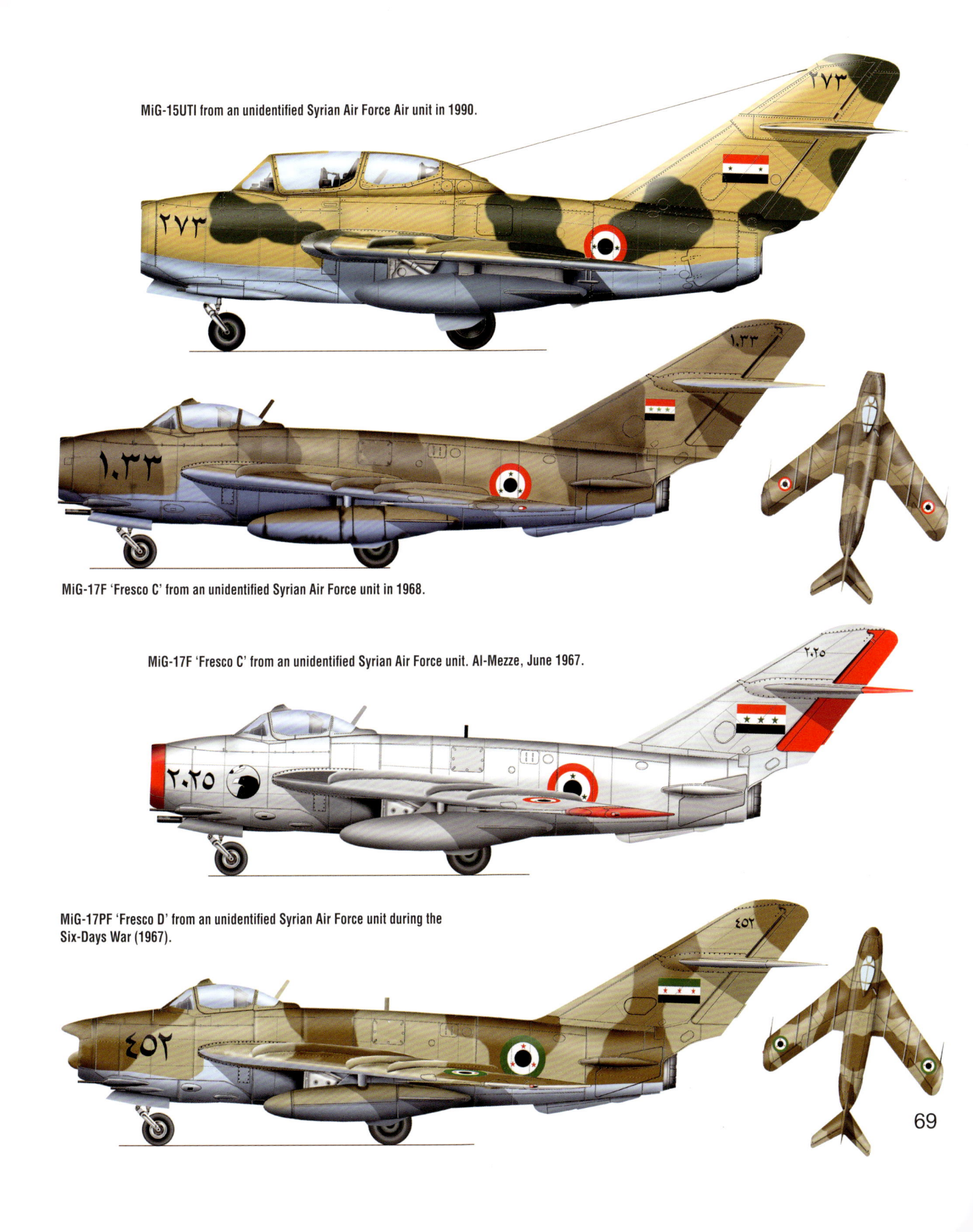

MiG-15UTI from an unidentified Syrian Air Force Air unit in 1990.

MiG-17F 'Fresco C' from an unidentified Syrian Air Force unit in 1968.

MiG-17F 'Fresco C' from an unidentified Syrian Air Force unit. Al-Mezze, June 1967.

MiG-17PF 'Fresco D' from an unidentified Syrian Air Force unit during the Six-Days War (1967).

69

# TANZANIA

Created in September 1964, the Tanzanian Air Force, the *Jeshi la Wananchi wa Tanzania* or JWTZ received two Shenyang FT-2s which remained in service until the middle of the eighties. In 1973, Tanzania received first twelve F-5s (the export version of the Shenyang J-5) then twenty-odd two-seat FT-5 trainers.

These planes were used for ground attack missions during the war between Tanzania and Uganda in 1978-79 which led to the downfall of the Ugandan president, Idi Amin Dada. In 2009 a certain number of these planes appeared to still be in service in the Tanzanian Air Force.

**MiG-15UTI of the *Jeshi la Wananchi wa Tanzania* (JWTZ – Tanzanian Air Force) at the beginning of the nineties.**

**MiG-17 of the JWTZ in 2004.**

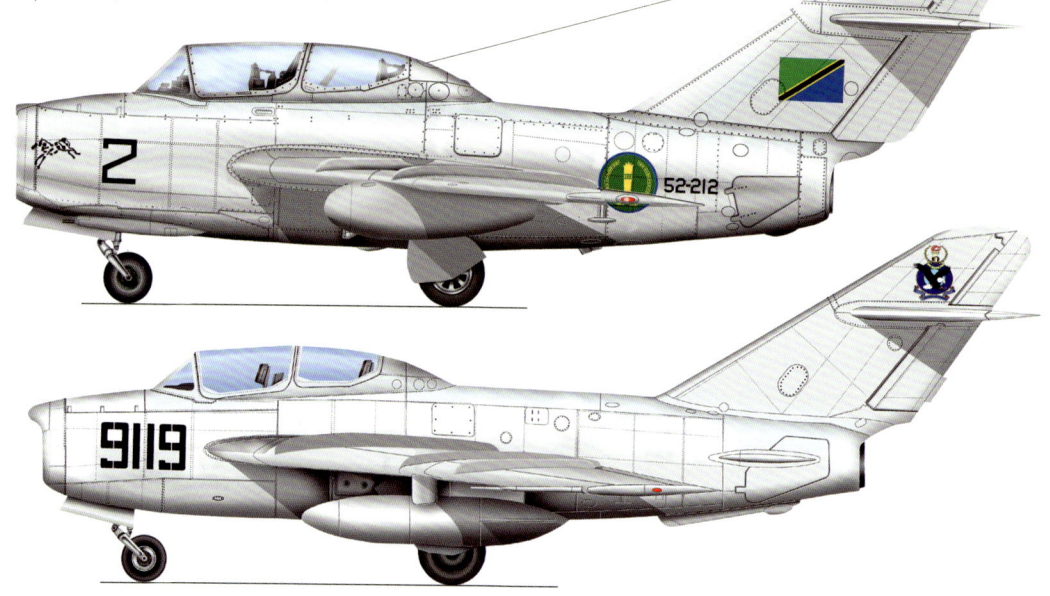

# UGANDA

It was in the middle of the sixties that the Ugandan Air Force (UAF) expanded considerably with aircraft deliveries coming both from the West and the Soviet Bloc, including two MiG-15UTI trainers and a dozen MiG-17F Fresco Cs which arrived in 1966 in Entebbe, the country's capital.

At the beginning of the seventies, the fact that the Ugandan government was planning to invade neighbouring Tanzania obliged Tanzania to support Ugandan dissidents exiled there and to back a *coup d'etat* in Kampala to overthrow the president, Idi Amin Dada.

In retaliation, the UAF bombed Tanzanian towns with its Mig-17Fs forcing the Tanzanian government to seek a ceasefire. In September 1972, the insurrectionists who were still active along the Tanzanian border were attacked, and Ugandan MiG-17Fs and Mig-21s bombed the Tanzanian towns of Bukoba and Mwanza. In the end, Ugandan troops helped by Libyan soldiers pushed the rebels back into Tanzania.

On 27 June 1976, a group of Palestinian terrorists hijacked an Air France Airbus A300 on its way from Tel Aviv to Paris and forced it to land at Entebbe. On 3 July, a unit of Israeli paratroopers liberated the passengers and destroyed four Ugandan MiG-17Fs on the ground.

In the summer of 1978, dissidents against Amin Dada's regime fled to Tanzania and joined the United Liberation Front which was preparing an offensive against Uganda for October 1978. Amin Dada launched a series of air raids against Tanzania with MiG-17s and Mig-21s and his troops crossed the border. In December, the Tanzanians succeeded in driving back the Ugandan troops and started progressing inside Uganda. In May 1979, several airfields were attacked by the Tanzanians and all the Ugandan MiG-17s and MiG-21s destroyed or captured.

Meanwhile some of the Ugandan military had defected and the Libyans had evacuated their troops. As for Idi Amin Dada, he fled to Libya then Saudi Arabia in April 1979. On the following 3 June the rest of the Ugandan army had to capitulate.

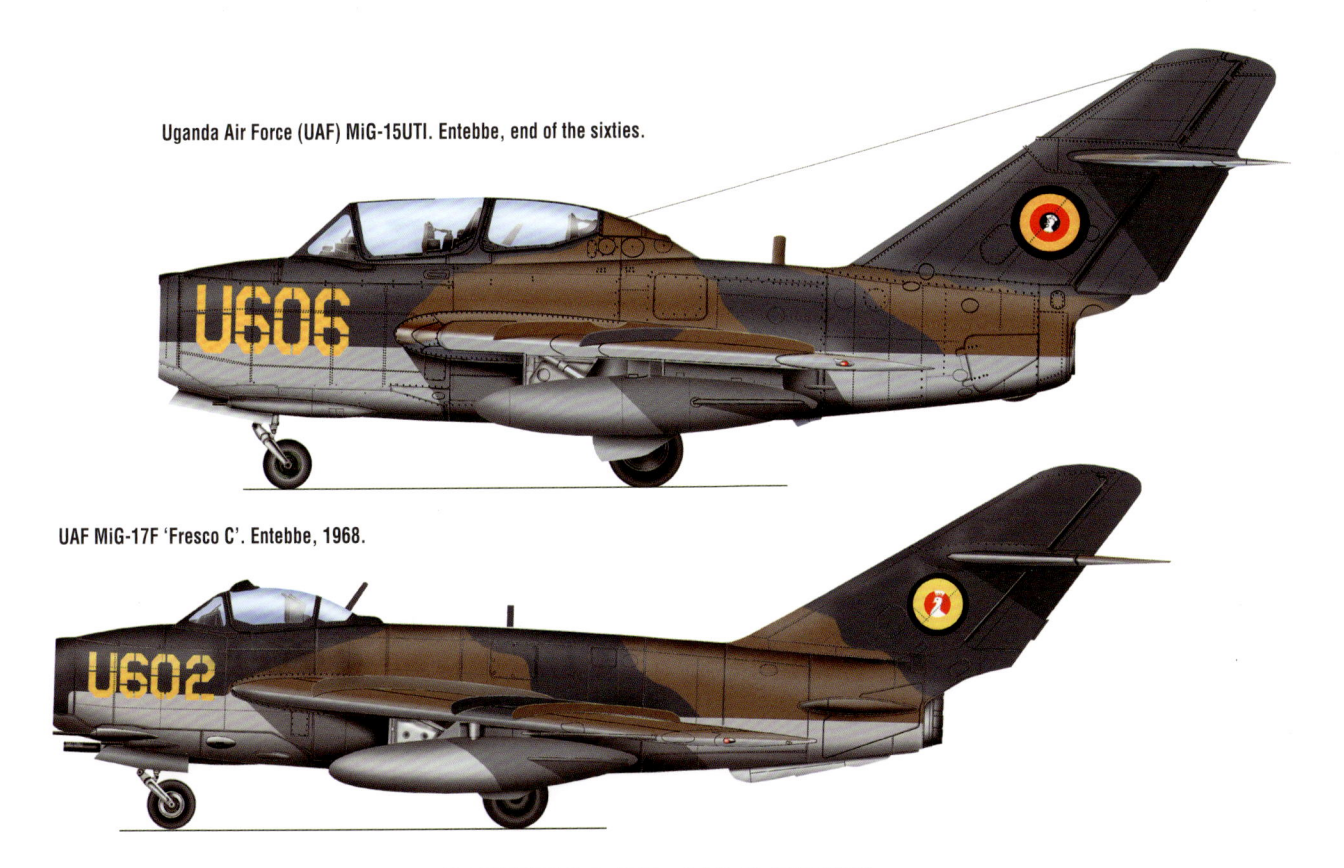

Uganda Air Force (UAF) MiG-15UTI. Entebbe, end of the sixties.

UAF MiG-17F 'Fresco C'. Entebbe, 1968.

# VIETNAM (NORTH)

The Vietnamese People's Air Force, the *Không Quân Nhân Dân Viet Nam*, received from both the Soviet Union and from China sixty or so MiG-15s and Shenyang J-2s together with some MiG-15UTIs and JJ-2s. The first MiG-17F/Shenyang F-5s were delivered by the Soviet Union and China in 1964-65, with North Vietnam receiving a total of 70 examples. These were operational during the Vietnam War during which they distinguished themselves particularly by their excellent handling even though faced with more modern, but also much heavier American fighters like the McDonnell Douglas F-4 Phantom II, the Vought F-8 Crusader or the Republic F-105 Thunderchief.

After 1966, the MiG-19s and MiG-21s were used alongside the MiG-17Fs which remained in front-line service until the end of the 1970s before being withdrawn from service during the following decade.

The MiG-17 aces during the Vietnam War were:
- Nguyen Van Bay (7 kills)
- Luu Huy Chao (6 kills)
- Le Hai (6 kills)
- Nguyen Nhat Chieu (6 kills).

**MiG-15UTI of the 910th Training Regiment, 1965.**

71

MiG-17 'Fresco A' from the 921st Fighter Regiment 'Sao Do'. 1967.

MiG-17 'Fresco C' of the 923rd Fighter Regiment 'Yen The', 1968. This plane has a wrap-around camouflage scheme.

MiG-17F 'Fresco C' from an unidentified unit of the North Vietnamese Air Force (NVAF). 1966. This plane has been painted entirely in 'air superiority' grey.

MiG-17F 'Fresco C' from an unidentified NVAF unit in 1966.

72

MiG-17F 'Fresco C' from an unidentified NVAF unit, 1968.

MiG-17F 'Fresco C' of the 921st Fighter Regiment 'Sao Do'. 1968.

MiG-17PF 'Fresco D' of the 921st Fighter Regiment 'Sao Do', 1965. This plane has been painted entirely in so-called 'air superiority' grey.

Shenyang JJ-5 of the 910th Training Regiment, 1967.

73

# YEMEN

The Soviet Union supplied both the Yemeni Arab Republic (North Yemen) and the People's Democratic Republic of Yemen (South Yemen), both countries receiving some MiG-15bis and MiG-15UTIs for training MiG-17 pilots. During the seventies, the North Yemen Air Force, the *al-Quwwat al-Jawwiya al-Yamaniya* and that of South Yemen, each received thirty-odd MiG-17F Fresco Cs. War broke out between the two countries in 1979, the South invading the North, obliging the latter to acquire new planes from the Soviet Union. The war ended in 1990 with the country reuniting under the name of the Republic of Yemen. At the time Yemen seemed still to have a certain number of MiG-15UTIs and MiG-17Fs.

**North Yemen Air Force MiG-15bis, 1990.**

# ZIMBABWE

The Air Force of Zimbabwe received a few Shenyang F-5s and two Shenyang FT-5 trainers leased by China at the end of the eighties. The two-seaters were used for converting F-7 pilots and in the middle of the nineties they were withdrawn from service and sent back to China. The F-5s were replaced by F-7M Airguards, the export version derived from the Shenyang J-7II, which itself was a variant of the MiG-21 produced in China.

**Air Force of Zimbabwe Shenyang FT-5, at the end of the 1980s.**